GRANDPA AND ANDY

Dr. Richard B. Liposky

MW00511327

Know the difference between right and wrong,
and always choose right.

All rights reserved. No part of this publication may be reproduced, stored in a retrieval system, or transmitted, in any form or by any means, electronic, mechanical, photocopying, recording, or otherwise, without the prior written consent of the author.

Copyright © 2017 by Dr. Richard B. Liposky
All rights reserved.

Green Ivy Publishing
1 Lincoln Centre
18W140 Butterfield Road
Suite 1500
Oakbrook Terrace IL 60181-4843
www.greenivybooks.com

Grandpa and Andy: A Grandfather's Handbook/Dr. Richard B. Liposky

ISBN: 978-1-946775-42-9
Ebook: 978-1-946775-43-6

Dedication

Dedicated to all my family. To Amy and George, to Angela and Rich, to Melissa and Mike, and to Michelle and Ruc. You have been the inspiration for this literary journey. To six grandchildren, Michelle and Andy, Cody and Braxton, Reece and Alex, who taught and trained me to be just Grandpa. Every step of the way, their Grandma Irene, who has tolerated and supported Grandpa's training for fifty years, patiently waited for the day when this literary masterpiece was finished. Patience, encouragement, love, and support made this journey possible. My hope is that the results of your support may help other Grandpas the way you have helped me.

Maybe even shorten their training time. Thanks to all of you. You have given me a puffed-up moment.

Endorsements

"Dr. Liposky has given us a memorable glimpse into a relationship of grandfather, mentor, and teacher. We all need to find and learn to be in this kind of relationship."
Jim Stovall
Bestselling Author *The Ultimate Gift*

Richard "Dick" Liposky incites through the words on these pages are rewarding and insightful. Dick illustrates how words and phrases can be teaching tools with measured results. An enjoyable read and lessons to be learned wrapped with a special gift: empathy.
Jody Victor
Business CEO and Leader, Entrepreneur, US Army Veteran, Grandfather

"Dr. Liposky once again has written a powerful book of inspiration and gratitude, every word ringing with truth, kindness and the beauty of the human spirit. It glows with inner light and practical wisdom. All of us can learn from his experiences.
Mark V. Migliore
Senior Vice President Sales
LaunchPad Media Management"

What a timely book! Dick Liposky has given us an important reminder that relationships matter, that the people we care about matter, that God has always focused on generational connections. You will learn valuable lessons for your life from this special book.
Ron Ball,
Speaker, best-selling author and host of the TV show Choose Greatness: Your Key to a Happier Life on TBN Salsa

Contents

Preface

Grandpa Training Session: It's Tough Being a Grandpa

We get one chance at being a mom and dad. We also get one chance at being a Grandpa. Since we have more kids to choose from, Grandpas have options. The other side is that since we have a bigger audience, we have two generations of critics.

Grandpas know how to deal with criticism. By the time he is a grandpa, he has been in training by Grandma for at least twenty years. Grandma is convinced that Grandpa is ready to graduate from her training program. After all, it would take too long to train another one.

Grandpa learns to get the last word in. "Yes, dear!" Grandma thinks he has finally learned. Grandpa calls it wisdom. Grandma thinks Grandpa is getting a little forgetful. Grandpa just remembers the important things. Everything else, Grandma will remind him!

So when the grandkids come around, they like to listen to Grandpa. He tells all the neat stories. He tells about why things happened in the past and what things are going to happen in the future. He has a story for almost every subject. Sometimes the story changes, but the subject is the same. Other times, the story is the same, but the subject changed. Never could figure out how he does that.

Grandpas have that little twinkle in their eye when the grandkids are around. He may have a two-day bristle, a missing tooth or two, and glasses that need to be cleaned. But he always has a smile. He always has a "Come here, give Grandpa a hug."

All three grandkids see Grandpa as the patriarch—a function of good parenting.

One commands recognition by correcting/teaching Grandpa
One gets recognition by listening to Grandpa
One needs recognition, so Grandpa listens.

One knows he's smart, intelligence is his sport, and study is his passion
One thinks he's smart, study is his sport, and athletics is his passion
One is not sure he is smart, drama is his sport, and relationship is his passion.

One sees his future as in control of people
One sees his future as leading people
One sees his future as helping people.

One sees Grandpa as wise but needs correction
One sees Grandpa as wise and worth listening too for now
One sees Grandpa as old, wise, funny, but needs reminding.

What about Grandpa?

- He sees all three boys with tremendous potential.
- He marvels at their skills, knowledge, and areas of interest.
- He's comforted in the knowledge that each has many individual, personal, but different gifts.
- He can't wait to see their accomplishments in the years to come.
- He sees three different leaders in their individual professions. Builders. Innovators. Motivators. Entrepreneurs.
- He's proud of their parents and the motivation and inspiration that they shared with the boys.
- His puffed-up moment will be when they look at wise

old grandpa and say, "For an old guy, he's still pretty cool," or "Remember when we shot a hole in his bird feeder, then blamed it on him. Said he probably did it himself and already forgot about it. He's old, you know!"

- His puffed-up moment will be when their mom and dad see the boys reach their dreams. When the boy turns to Mom and Dad, smile, and say, "Thanks, Mom and Dad."

Introduction

A professor once remarked that I didn't ask questions; I asked answers. He said that when I asked a question, I just wanted to confirm that I knew the answer. One day we had a chance to talk. He explained that news reporters ask questions more often to get confirmation rather than information. If they learned how to ask questions, they would get more information and be able to write a more factual and accurate report.

He said that reporters ask questions with an agenda in mind. They want a story, not the facts. If you wanted directions to a restaurant, you would want simple directions. You don't need all the scenic details, bumps in the road, and names of all the people you might meet along the way. Just give me the facts.

The professor turned out to be a great mentor in my business and professional career. I learned to be a better listener. The look over his glasses was all I needed to see. I learned to listen in order to get information and not to respond. I learned how to seek knowledge, how to ask questions in order to get information, not confirmation.

We need to go back and listen to our children. Their questions are pure (often profound) and based on a certain natural curiosity. They don't ask what we are having for dinner. They just want to know, "When can we eat?" Just the facts. This story is about the simple questions that children ask. They see something, and they ask a question. They don't have an agenda other than, "Keep it short, Grandpa. I don't need a lecture."

Grandpas are very special people in our family. They are looked up to for all the answers, but they know that with all their experiences, they still don't have all the answers. What grandpas do have is life experience, both personal and by observation of others, which translates into wisdom.

Being a grandfather gives us a second chance at being a dad without all the day-to-day duties of being a dad. Fathers get one chance at being a dad. They get their training from watching their own father. How did Dad lead, teach, and support the family? He established the moral foundation for his children. He supported them when things were tough and coached them to succeed. His relationship with Mom, with his parents, and with siblings would be an example for his children. He set the example for the family. Good or bad, the lesson was taught and would be used in the next generation.

Even though this book is about grandpas, there can't be a grandpa without a grandma. This may be a simplification of the family unit, but I believe that the two parents make up the family leadership. They complement and support each other and must step up just as any team members support the rest of the team. It's not just another game; it is the only game. Parents get one chance to raise their children. They want to get it right.

In those circumstances when there is a single-parent family unit, the responsibility to lead, teach, and support is on that single parent. In those cases, the grandparents can be helpful, but the responsibility still rests on the parent. As tough as it might be, it can be done.

We hear every day of children from a single-parent family unit that went on to become successful. Conversely, we hear of children that blame their failures in life on their early and current family circumstances. We are where we are today based on the decisions that we have made in the past. The family unit, two parents or a single parent, is only one element in the development of children. It is the place where they learn. It is the classroom, one teacher or two. What is taught in the classroom is the foundation. How the child uses that information will determine and distinguish the child's future.

What is a Grandpa?

This is a story about a grandfather and his grandson Andy. You may know an Andy and likely have a grandfather in your life. He is just a typical grandpa. But grandpas are interesting birds. They sit, they listen, and they decide when to talk. They understand that there are two or more sides to every argument. They understand that perception may cloud wisdom. They understand that their opinion is based on knowledge and wisdom, but that wisdom does not always prevail. And they understand that if their wisdom does not prevail, the consequences of one's actions are borne by the actor.

Sometimes Grandpa's message is a few words. Sometimes the message involves the whole lecture with a PowerPoint presentation. Well, maybe not that intense, but at least the whole lecture. Grandpas are beyond trying to impress people. They know who they are. They look to understand people and see where they might be able to help them, if they'll listen. They try to anticipate the challenges that their grandchildren will face and give them the tools to persist.

What is neat about being a grandpa is that he was raised by a mom and dad, he has raised a mom and dad himself, with grandma's help, and has nearly completed the grandfather's post-grad training program taught by grandma. He has learned that he can get the last word in, so long as it is "Yes, dear."

Grandpas get a second chance at being a dad. Dads only get one chance to learn how to be a dad. Now, kids have two grandpas from whom to learn. It's not a competition. It's called the diversification of wisdom. The kids can decide who is "more" right. That's why, from grandpas' perspective, the moral, ethical, and family values should coincide. The knowledge, experience, and wisdom of each grandpa should support and complement the family values lessons.

Children will relate, respect, and respond to Grandpa as a reflection of their parents' respect for Grandpa. The author sees this in children who come for treatment. Even though they may be sick or in pain, some children are respectful while others are commanding and disrespectful. If they are that way with a doctor, even though a stranger but someone who can help them, then they are likely to act that way with most adults with whom they encounter. They learn this from their parents. If the parents are teaching the right values, the child gets the help that he needs, and he is most likely to listen to Grandpa.

D.Mata 2014

Chapter 1

Mixed Emotions

Grandpa sat in his chair quietly watching the events unfold. He had received a CD from his grandson Andy's friend, and he was anxious to take a look.

Dover Air Force Base, Delaware, came across the screen and a military formation was assembling. The airplane was huge. The tail section slowly raised, and four soldiers in full dress uniforms stood at the top of the ramp. Behind them, rows of coffins could be seen. What was this? Grandpa's heart sank. No. This can't be.

"Andy! Andy!" he shouted at the TV.

Slowly, each coffin, draped with the American flag, was brought down to the tarmac. The soldiers were at attention, saluting their fallen comrades. One by one. Grandpa just stared at the screen. Not a word. He thought, they gave their all and a salute from their comrades in arms was all the thanks they needed. To them it was worth it.

The Other Side

Grandpa finally saw the other side. In Vietnam, he was on the AF surgical team in the Mekong Delta and saw the carnage of war. In Saigon, he saw truckloads of coffins, every Friday, waiting to go to the flight line. They were to be loaded on the C-141 transport planes and taken back stateside to waiting, grieving families.

Every day, the dispensary processed 50 to 100 wounded soldiers who were the lucky ones. They were also headed for the flight line, but their destination would be to military hospitals for treatment and rehabilitation.

Seeing the video at Dover and the flag-draped coffins brought back a lot of memories. Andy and Grandpa had talked about Vietnam on many occasions. As Andy became a teenager, he wanted to know more about the war. In school, the teachers taught them that the Vietnam War was wrong and that the United States should never have been involved. Grandpa would get so upset.

One time Andy asked, "Grandpa, why would the government send us to battle if we weren't supposed to be there? There were fifty thousand men and women killed and hundreds of thousands wounded in that war."

"Andy, let me tell you about war," he said.

Grandpa on War

Grandpa explained that we have had wars ever since our country was formed. There are books on warfare and books on individual wars. Grandpa didn't talk too much about why wars were fought. He just felt that if we send our men and women to fight on behalf of our country, they should be given all the support needed to do their job. He said that soldiers and their generals fight wars, but politicians start and end them. It is easy for politicians to start a war. They don't have any skin in the game. If they had to lead from the front, their attitude would change.

Grandpa remembered a president who had tears for people caught in domestic gun violence but wouldn't acknowledge the wounded or deceased soldiers he commanded. Politicians end wars when it is politically expedient, when it is more comfortable to talk than to fight.

He also recalled another president, George Bush, who took his staff to the Vietnam memorial late one night just before he gave the order to start the first Middle East war involving Iraq and Kuwait. He was a president who was a WWII vet and understood the sacrifice that he was asking these young men and women to make. He had tears in his eyes before he sent them into battle.

When Politicians Fight Wars

Grandpa said that in Vietnam, they would drop leaflets announcing when the B-52 bombers were going to drop their bombs. The enemy fighters were not allowed to read these leaflets.

The leaflet police would watch, and if an enemy fighter picked up a leaflet, they were put on probation and not allowed to participate in the war for at least a year.

The civilians were allowed to read the leaflets, knew when and where the bombing would occur, and could seek safety. The enemy fighters, because they weren't allowed to read the leaflets, had to stay in place and wait for the bomb to drop on them.

Andy just shook his head. "Grandpa, you're kidding me, right?"

"Yes, Andy. The villages did not have leaflet police. We just trusted that the enemy would not read them."

"If you told them when and where you were going to bomb, then how did you kill the enemy fighters?" he asked.

"We didn't. But we probably scared them."

Grandpa's pitch was that if you send a soldier to fight, let him do the job you sent him to do. Don't put him in harm's way and then tie his hands to fight. Grandpa was concerned that our war in the Middle East was not too different than Vietnam. We put men and women in harm's way, but the "rules of engagement," written by the bureaucrats for the politicians, prevented them from doing the job that we sent them to do. And just like the leaflet program in Vietnam, the enemy fighters in Iraq, Syria, and Afghanistan were not allowed to read our rules of engagement.

The enemy fighters were not allowed to search the Internet that we built, with the technology that we developed, with the computers and phones made in the United States, to print out and distribute our rules of engagement. They were not allowed to know that if they shot at one of our soldiers, the soldier could not shoot back until he could identify the enemy fighter and make sure that there were no women or children that could get hurt during a firefight.

The enemy fighters were not allowed to know that if they launched a rocket from an area in a town and it killed one of our serviceman, we had to make sure that civilians were safe before we engaged the fighters. We explained that we wanted the enemy fighters to stay in place until we could engage them. We just had to be sure that the women and children were out of the way.

Andy just shook his head. He was sixteen now, and he could understand Grandpa's humor.

"That sounds like the leaflet program all over again."

"Same thing, except now we don't have to drop leaflets. We just give them the website where they can look it up on their own."

"Was that more humor, Grandpa?" Andy asked. "Sadly, yes," he replied.

Andy chose to serve his country.

When Andy joined ROTC in college, he asked Grandpa if it was a good decision. It was a puffed-up moment for Grandpa. He was proud of Andy. His country would be proud of him.

Grandpa and Andy talked about a lot of things, but as Andy learned more about military tactics and strategies, he began to understand war. The *Art of War* by Sun Tzu was a popular reference. "The supreme art of war is to subdue the enemy without fighting" and "Know thy self, know thy enemy. A thousand battles, a thousand victories" were Grandpa's favorite quotes from the book.

He talked about being responsible as a soldier and representative of our country. It was an honor to wear our uniform. It was something that every soldier wears with pride. The soldier's chest is strong with muscle, but it's true strength, dedication and determination, comes from the pride and honor to serve. It's not until you wear the uniform that you will understand. With each new uniform that Andy put on, he understood. Grandpa was right. You had to wear it to know.

Grandpa was eighty-six now. He didn't keep up with things like he used too. Why did Andy's friend send him the video? Why didn't Andy send it or even call him? What was so important about all these caskets draped with our flag?

Chapter 2

Andy's Grandpa

Grandpa was never short of words of wisdom. Even if he wasn't sure of the wisdom, he could be creative. But he never wanted to mislead. When he talked about growing up, he had a whole list of things that he thought young people should learn. Andy heard them over and over. These are some of his favorites.

1. Learn to take and accept responsibility.
2. Learn to think outside the box.

3. Learn to deal with success and failure. Make success and failure learning experiences. Build on your successes and the success of others. Learn from your failures and the failures of others.
4. Learn to respect the hand that feeds you and suspect the hand that needs you.
5. Learn to help those who want to be helped, who are willing to try to help themselves. One working for two is harder that two working for one.
6. Learn that you get what you sow. You harvest what you plant.
7. Learn that people who lie have to have good memories. People who tell the truth remember events and circumstances rather than fiction and fantasy.

Growing Up in the City: Learning to Be Tough Was Tough

New Castle was a medium-size mill town with industry that grew out of WWII. Machine shops, foundries, glassworks, and pottery were the main industries. Eastern European cultures were dominant, followed by the Italians, Irish, Germans, and a few Asians and Jews. Even though there was competition on the ball fields and bowling alleys, and there was no shortage of ethnic commentary; everyone seems to get along. They had to. They all worked together.

There weren't any gangs as we know them today, but the Mafia was alive and well. They extracted their tax from whomever they chose. If there was a good thing from their presence—and the term *good* is used loosely—it's that they kept the peace. This underworld culture was entrenched from the mill towns around Pittsburgh, up through the Beaver and Shenango valleys to and beyond Youngstown. Although in different forms, this culture persisted well into the eighties.

The churches were also ethnocentric. The Italians and Irish had their catholic churches, and everyone else went to St.

Mary's. Most catholic churches had their own grade schools, so the kids rarely interacted outside the schools. High school brought them all together. Most of the children participated in basketball, baseball, and football or music. The mill towns did not have much interest in golf, tennis, squash, or symphony.

Their own mom and all the neighborhood moms looked after the children. Most moms were at home raising the kids. The dads were working in the factory. The famous and dreaded words were "Wait till your father gets home and I tell him what you did." If you misbehaved, tramped on a neighbor's flowers, stole a big red tomato from their garden, they simply told your mom and everything else was history. "Wait till your dad gets home!" Keep in mind that Mom still used the wooden spoon, a twist of the ear, and the "Go to your room" torture technique for minor offenses, but Dad was the disciplinarian.

As a six-year-old, Grandpa walked two blocks to Washington Street to catch the city bus. For nine cents, he would ride downtown and then walk two blocks to St. Mary's school. After school, he would have music lessons or music theory class and then catch the bus home. (Today, would you let your six-year-old walk the streets, take a city bus unaccompanied, and not have contact with him until that evening when he walked in the door?)

When Grandpa was ten, a savings bond matured, and he bought a paper route. To increase his profit, he would walk to the New Castle news offices and pick up his papers, then take his papers on the bus. He saved money on the delivery charges, but lost money as he learned to pitch pennies with the other paperboys while waiting for the papers to come off the press. Grandpa (GP) made one of his early business decisions when he gave up on using his skill pitching pennies as a source of revenue. He quit pitching pennies and carrying his papers on the bus. He paid the delivery truck driver the penny a paper to drop them off at a corner near his route. It was a net gain.

It was not easy, but that was life in the city. Grandpa's dad, Andy's great-grandpa (GGP), was a good athlete and a go-getter. He was tough, scrappy, highly competitive, a leader, and the life of the party. He wanted GP to be tough, but GP really didn't care to fight. GGP would instigate fights with the neighbor kids to get GP to fight. It usually ended in embarrassment to GGP, as GP would often just walked away. GP learned at an early age to pick his battles.

GP would rather build things with an Erector Set, build model airplanes, or cook. GP would see a machine and then try to build it with the Erector Set. He accumulated more and more Erector parts from relatives who were amazed at his talent. One adventure was when he built a life-size cockpit for a rocket ship that he saw in a comic book. He took a sandwich and glass of milk with him and sat in the cockpit waiting to take off. He woke up an hour later with the imprint of the sandwich on his face. He was still in the cockpit in the attic.

He built model airplanes and decided to sell them to his friends. He could buy ten kits for a dollar and get two free. The original plan was to sell the two free kits for fifty cents each and he would get his kits free. When there were no takers, GP changed his strategy and decided to build the planes and sell them for twenty-five cents each. He would net two dollars on the deal. There would be plenty of money to buy more kits, make more planes, and become a millionaire in the aircraft industry. GP ended up with twelve planes neatly arranged in the attic and a real need to develop a new strategy. He learned that you should understand the market before you open your store. Don't try to sell winter coats in the desert and don't try to sell airplanes to kids who only want to play baseball. Building things served GGP well a few years later on the farm.

GP the Musician

GGP liked to sing and dance. His vision was GP playing the accordion at a party. He saw GP playing while the people sung along or danced the polka. GP's vision was keeping his eyes on the music so that Sister Mary Joseph wouldn't slap his fingers with her pointer. Sister taught GP to play the piano, not the accordion. Sister taught GP to play Mozart and Chopin and not "Roll Out the Barrel" or the "Clarinet Polka." Who sings to Mozart? GP learned to play the cello. Did you ever see people singing along to a cello? Neither did GGP. Under great pressure, Sister Mary Joseph consented to GP learning a popular song, "How Much Is That Doggie in the Window" and "That's Amore." These songs didn't bring audiences to the door, but it was a compromise for GGP.

When the family moved to the farm, GP joined the band in the Plain Grove country school. They didn't have a need for the cello; they didn't have a cello. GP played the piano in orchestra and learned to play the drums in the marching band. Again, they wouldn't let him play the piano in the marching band. They claimed it would take too many kids to push it up and down the streets. GP learned that in a parade, the drummers played all the time. When the band played music, the drummers played the music. When the band finished the song, the drummer played cadence as they marched.

He learned to keep in step and in line. The high school was in a small college town in the center of a large Amish population. The Amish sent their children to one of eight one-room schoolhouses throughout the district. The children only went to the eighth grade. They never went on to high school. Horses and buggies were common along the roads and in New Wilmington. GP learned that when the band marched in town, he kept his eyes on the line in front. If he noticed a bend in the line at one particular spot, that bend meant that a horse had left a deposit on the street. Keeping the marching line straight would mean kicking the crap off your shoes and later riding bare feet on the band bus. GP learned to always know where you are and where you are going at all times.

GP's New Business Strategy

When the family moved to the farm, GP sold his paper route for $100. He had savings from the paper sales, two cents a paper, plus the sale of the route. GP was going into the cattle business of which he and no one in the family had any knowledge or experience. So where did the family experience and knowledge come from? Was it in their genes, or jeans? One of Andy's great-great-grandpas (GGGP) was raised on a small subsistence farm in Austria and worked as a child on a farm before coming to America. He survived by eating the raw eggs that the "hens broke." He ate the eggs for survival. The hens that broke too many eggs were headed for the soup pot. He tried to spread the egg breaks around in order to save the hens. When he came to America, GGGP would not eat eggs. It was part of the family lore.

When GGGP was eleven, he boarded a boat by himself and came to America. He survived on the boat by eating the meals of the people who were too seasick to eat, which may explain why he never got on a boat after he put his feet on the ground in America. His older stepbrother was already in America and helped him get started in the new life. At fourteen, he lied about his age and got a job in the coal mine. At eighteen he left the mine after an altercation with the superintendent and went to work in the steel mill. GGGP worked in the mill until he retired at sixty-five.

Andy's other GGGP came from Russia. He came from a small farm but only applied his farming skills to the family garden. He started as a street car conductor in Rankin, a steel mill community south of Pittsburgh. When he lost the brakes on a steep hill and scared him and all the passengers, he decided to go to work in the mills. He worked in the wire mill until his retirement.

During the 1930s and 1940s, most people had backyard gardens. They grew all their fruits and vegetables for summer consumption and storage and canning for the winter. Everyone in the family had a garden of some sort. Some had a chicken coop for eggs. No one in the family had any cattle or hogs for milk or meat. That was the extent of GP's family agricultural background. Then, at age eleven, Grandpa launched his cattle business. Grandpa learned that he must surround himself with people who know what he doesn't know, which, at that time, was just about everyone.

Grandpa Learns the Farming Business

Farming for GP and the family was a combination of business and survival. GP invested his money in a cow, her calf, and a young heifer. His dad invested in four Hereford heifers and a bull. GP also bought five bred gilts and a boar. The family had chickens for meat and eggs. The cows produced enough milk and cheese. The beef cattle provided all the meat and a couple of extra head to sell. Before long, GP had so many cows and more milk than they could use or even give away.

When the Amish opened a cheese plant, GP separated the curd to sell and fed the whey to the young hogs. Not only did GP have more cows, but his hog herd was growing rapidly. The pigs farrowed two to three times a year. He shipped hogs to the market and provided all the pork (smoked hams, chops, and sausage) for the family. Now he was in the cattle, hog, and cheese business. The money from selling the curds to the cheese plant paid for the seed and fertilizer needed for the spring planting.

The large livestock population demanded a steady and nutritious supply of food year-round. That meant pastures during the summer and stored hay and grains for the winter. He and GGP had to learn the production and storage process. GP was caught between GGP who thought he knew and the neighbor farmers who knew. GP was planting corn one spring, and the neighbor came over and asked why he was planting corn. GP told him because his dad told him to plant the corn. The farmer explained that the soil was too wet to plant and that the seed would rot rather than germinate. But Dad told GP to plant, so he continued to plant. None of the corn, short of a few stalks, in the whole field came up. They lost the seed, the fertilizer, the time, and the fuel.

GGP was upset. GP must have done something wrong. GP knew what had happened but couldn't say. Sometimes it doesn't pay to argue just to prove a point. GGP had to learn from the people he trusted, not from a fourteen-year-old son. But GP learned an important lesson. When you feel it's wrong, get more information. When you know it is wrong, don't do it just to prove that it is wrong.

> Know the difference between right and wrong, and always choose right.

Funds were limited on the farm. A lot of the equipment had been maintained by repair rather than replacement. GP had some engineering skills as a young teenager. GGP would have him draw out pieces of equipment that they saw at the farm equipment and supply stores. GP enjoyed it. It was like playing with his Erector Set years ago, but this was for real.

GGP was a machinist in the mill, so he could make most of the parts. Once GP had it on paper to scale, GGP would just follow the drawing. They built a lot of equipment and saved a lot of money. The colors were based on the cheapest can of paint that they could buy. The other farmers always wondered where GGP and GP got their equipment. They just couldn't recognize the brand. There were many learning experiences on the farm, but it all worked out. GP grew up and learned about the business side of farming. The family grew up and grew together, later taking what they had learned and applying it to building an eighteen-hole public golf course.

Throughout those years with GGP, GP heard over and over, "Get a good education." *Get an education, get a good job, and then go out and work for yourself.* GP would repeat it over and over to all his grandchildren. After a while, they may have become tired of hearing it, but if they got the message, it was worth it. So how did it work out for GP?

Grandpa Goes to the Big City ... to College

About the time that GP was headed to college, the Russians had launched the Sputnik satellite. It was almost patriotic that we needed more engineers to get a man on the moon. GP wanted to be an engineer. The family could not afford Carnegie Tech University, so GP enrolled at Duquesne University. He sold his cattle and hogs to pay for tuition.

The first year was great. GP did what he was told. He attended class, listened, and studied. It paid off. Straight As. The second year was a disaster. Because the first year was a success, GP felt he knew more than his professors and, therefore, didn't need to attend classes. His strategy was to just show up for the tests. He was working nearly full-time and had a girlfriend. Sounded like a good strategy. At the end of the first semester of his second year, he had successfully flunked all his courses. GP learned that *when you think you know, you probably don't. And when you think you know everything, you don't.*

GP's uncle Rich was the first member of the family to go to college. After serving in the USAF, he went to dental school. During the summer after the GP's first year at Duquesne, GP spent some time watching Uncle Rich treating patients. GP decided he wanted to become a dentist. Based on his excellent first year, he was given early acceptance into dental school. Based on the disastrous current semester, his acceptance was revoked. And *when you know you know everything, it's time to sit down, shut up, and listen.*

The saddest day was when GP told his father that he had flunked all his classes and that he didn't make it into dental school. GGP had been so proud of his son going to college and getting accepted into dental school after only two years of college instead of four. GGP just put his head down. There wasn't any anger as GP thought might come. The disappointment overwhelmed the anger. In a soft, quivering voice, with tears streaming down his face, he told GP that he would see if he could pull some strings and get him a job in the mill. A college education in the family would have to wait for the next generation.

GP saw a part of GGP that he had never seen before. He had hurt his father. This man was a fighter, and his son caused more hurt than a punch, a knife, or a bullet. It struck at his heart. He put his hand on GGP's shoulder and told him that he would never let him down again. GP was determined to make things right. He thought his strategy was wrong, but he didn't get help. He chose and then did the wrong thing. It cost him a whole year of college, but he learned the lessons of accountability and responsibility.

A new strategy was now in place. No more girlfriend. Attend all classes. Study every night. And continue to work nearly full-time for survival. If what he was doing didn't help him get into dental school, he would not do it. GP had exhausted what little financial help he had received from the family. If he wanted to move forward, he would have to do it on his own. At the end of the third year in college, GP had straight As again. He was immediately accepted into dental school.

Andy's Grandpa

Grandpa's Lessons from Failure

The lessons of failure, disappointment, and irresponsibility paid dividends. GP worked nights in the hospital while in dental school. He was selected as a research assistant where he learned research techniques. That knowledge allowed him to conduct research throughout his professional career. GP graduated in the top five of his class. He was accepted for a USAF internship, offered to only twenty-seven out of the five thousand graduates in the country. He was determined. Never again would he choose wrong over right.

GP graduated, got married, and went on active duty in the USAF in the month of June 1966. The military opened the doors to a new life. He ended up in Vietnam and was assigned to an air force surgical team. There, he had exposure to some of the worst facial injuries. His teammates helped him administer to the wounded. He headed the medical civic action (Medcap) teams that went into the hamlets to help the civilians caught up in the war.

Unbeknown to GP, this experience was what some professionals in the hospitals were looking for in order to start a comprehensive facial reconstructive surgery training program. He was selected for a five-year training program, which would include oral surgery, plastic surgery, ENT surgery, and anesthesia. Five more years. But now he had to consider his wife and a young family. The program would introduce many new surgical techniques and procedures. Clinical research experience was essential.

But a new evil began to show its ugly head. Professional politics. Professional jealousy. This was focused on the founders of the program, but it would eventually spread to all the young men and women associated with the program. Over time, it all dissipated. Why? Because what GP and all his colleagues were doing was the right thing to do. *Know the difference between right and wrong, and always choose right. Right might seem harder, but it is the best path to follow.*

GP never got the farming bug out of his system. After selling the patent rights for an invention of a medical device, he took the proceeds and, while starting his surgery practice, went back into farming. Now he thought he knew about the business of farming. He found that he still had more to learn. *When you think you know everything, you don't.* After a few years of successes and failures on the farms, he opted to focus his skills and talents on research and surgery.

The profession was changing as new surgical techniques, technologies, and methods of health-care delivery were introduced. New surgical procedures became state of the art and the foundation for future new procedures. GP learned that the only sure thing was change. If we learn to embrace it, we grow. If we resist it, it will pass us by.

By nature, people tend to resist change. They like things the way they are. Change requires a learning experience, and most people will shy away from a learning experience. But it is interesting that even though they may resist change, they will embrace the benefits of change. The smart phone—kids won't put it down, and old people won't pick it up. Three remotes for the TV versus one on/off button.

Throughout GP's professional career as a facial surgeon, he continued to conduct clinical research. He reported his findings at national and international symposiums. He published many professional articles and even wrote books. He kept a notebook with his thoughts on many different subjects. He kept copies of all the talks that he had given and notes about the audiences. He said he never wanted to give the same talk to the same audience.

At one time he hosted a weekly radio program and had

numerous TV appearances. He worked with young doctors during their training and taught students and practicing doctors surgical techniques as well as sound business principles. He participated in humanitarian missions in war zones around the world.

Over the years, GP had been busy. He doesn't get around as much as before. Walking is preferred over running. Riding is preferred over driving. Reading rather than writing. And prefers just listening rather than talking. He sits back with a smile enjoying the "Gs": Grandma, grandkids, great-grandkids, golf, and gardening. Now, more than ever, he gets to see the results of the teachings of four generations in the faces of the fifth and sixth generations. He passed on these teachings to benefit future generations, and he never let his dad down.

Grandpa's Legacy

1. Know the difference between right and wrong, and always choose right.
2. Be accountable for your actions. Accept responsibility.
3. Never stop learning. When you quit learning, you start dying.
4. Change the things you can change. Don't worry about the thing that can't be changed.
5. Help the people who want to be helped. Don't worry about the people who don't want to be helped.

It might have been his research training or just his personality, but GP always kept notes on his presentations and travels. He recorded thoughts, observations, and feelings as he interacted with patients and people from around the world. These often became the inspiration and subjects of his presentations. He said he never wanted to give the same talk to the same audience.

Andy's Grandpa

When GP had a chance to sit with the kids, he would take out his notebooks and tell them to pick a page number. The kids loved it. They tried to guess what was on the page. It always meant a story. Sometimes the story was not even on the page, but GP would come up with one. As the kids got older, GP would just tell stories. Some were funny, some were scary, and some were exciting, but he would always have a little message at the end. Something that just made you think. Hmm!

"Oh, Grandpa. You're just kidding, aren't you?"

D.Mata 2014

Chapter 3

Proud Moments That We Don't Talk About

Andy and GP were walking among the flowerbeds. GP was proud of the patterns of color from the different flowers. Andy didn't quite appreciate the work that went in to producing the patterns, but he always enjoyed the many colors. It seemed like every time he visited GP, the flowers had created different patterns. GP knew all the flowers, when they would bloom, and how they would complement each other.

GP bragged that he had something blooming from the first crocus in March to the last mums after the frost in November.

Proud Moments That We Don't Talk About

The waves of color moved across the grounds throughout the year. As one variety died off, the next started to bloom. How did GP make that happen? It must have been magic.

Andy knew a few comments about the flower usually resulted in a guided tour. Grandpa told him that when he went to the big city to start college, he grew lettuce and tomatoes in a box on the windowsill. He said when he was in the air force, he grew lettuce and radishes when they told him he had to plant flowers. GP was a little stubborn. He didn't like them telling him that he had to plant flowers. The funny thing was that the sergeant who inspected his flowers didn't recognize the difference. He complimented GP on his nice rows of lettuce and radish "flowers."

This particular visit, Andy seemed a little distant. As they walked among the flowers, Andy didn't seem to be absorbing all of GP's flower wisdom. Andy seemed to be just tagging along. At one point, GP turned around, and Andy was just staring at him.

"What's up, Andy? You seem distracted. Are you OK?" GP asked.

"I guess I'm OK. Grandpa, why am I not supposed to ask you about the war?" Andy replied. "Why are you not allowed to talk about the war?'

Grandpa was surprised. "What brought that on?" he asked.

"I know you were a soldier and that you fought in the Vietnam War. Mom and Dad told me that I should not ask you about it. They said you don't talk about it much and that you might cry."

Grandpa just looked at Andy. Little Andy might not be little anymore. His grandson is growing up. He's asking the tough questions. What prompted Andy to ask GP about the war? Why now, in the garden, talking about flowers like we always do?

Proud Moments That We Don't Talk About

Grandpa did serve in Vietnam. He saw and experienced a lot of things, but when he came back to the States, he couldn't talk about them. The war was unpopular with some people. The vets were not allowed to talk about their service. Being a patriot and serving your country, although noble and the right thing to do, could bring on insults and disdain.

Andy was thirteen now and almost up to GP's shoulders. Grandpa turned and just went over to Andy, grabbed him, and gave him one of his big bear hugs.

"Andy, don't ever be afraid to ask me a question. That's what I'm here for."

Sometimes, when Andy came to visit, Andy would find GP out in the yard, sitting on his bench. He would be reading a book or working his way through the latest *Wall Street Journal*. Now, GP took Andy over to the bench. Andy was starting to get a little worried. GP wasn't saying anything.

"Andy, why did you ask me that question? Are you worried about me?" he asked.

"I'm not worried about you, Grandpa. We have been studying the Vietnam War in school, and my teacher Mr. Callahan told us that the war was wrong and that we should not have fought that war.

"My teacher told us that the Vietnam War was a bad war and that we should never have fought in that war. He said that there were many people who protested the war, and some people even left the country so that they would not have to fight in that war. He said that the draft was wrong and that we should not have sent our young men to Vietnam to get killed. He said that we killed many men and women and children who were not even fighting in the war but who just happened to live in that country. He said that some of our soldiers were actually baby killers."

Grandpa was speechless. He put his head down and just stared at the ground. Andy looked over at Grandpa and looked up into his eyes. Big tears were starting to form. He wondered whether Mom and Dad were right. Maybe he should not have asked Grandpa about the war.

Grandpa looked up and hesitated. "When I hear stuff like that, Andy, it really hurts inside. I really want to grab that teacher and set him straight. Regardless of whether we could have done things differently, every guy and gal that went there, went there because their country asked them to go. And, Andy, some never came back. We should be thanking them rather than judging them. Sorry, Andy, it just bothers me."

"Why would Mr. Callahan say that the war was wrong if our country asked our soldiers to go to war?" Andy asked.

"Things are not always that simple, Andy," Grandpa went on.

"If you have two people who disagree, there are only two opinions to be decided. But if you have ten people who disagree with ten other people, each group of ten has to agree among themselves to disagree with the other ten. Ten members of a team have to agree to work together toward a common goal in order to engage and defeat that other team. Getting everyone in a country to agree is nearly impossible."

Grandpa explained that even during the Civil War, there were people in the North and South who opposed the war. Yet millions were called and fought, and more than five hundred thousand men were killed during that war. The Vietnam War was not any different. Some people disagreed with the war, but the country, the people we elected to speak for us, decided that the war was the right thing to do. That meant sending our young men and women to battle. That also meant that when we send them, we support them, and take care of them when they return.

Proud Moments That We Don't Talk About

Grandpa slowly looked up at Andy, tears streaking down his face, and his voice was crackling. "Andy, 58,000 young men and women died in the Vietnam War. From August 1964 to March of 1973, Andy, 8,700,000 men and women served in that war. And, Andy, every one of those people who served was asked to serve by their country. And they accepted that mission because the people in this country asked them to do so.

"When I hear you talk about your teacher, it makes me sick inside. There were 500,000 of us in the country when Grandpa was there. I saw the tractor-trailer loads of coffins waiting to be loaded onto airplanes. Soldiers that were being delivered to their families in a flag-draped casket. At the end of each day, our dispensary was filled with wounded young men and women who would be shipped out in the morning to hospitals in the Philippines, Japan, and stateside. In the morning, the dispensary was empty, but by six o'clock that evening, it was filled again with wounded soldiers.

"The wounded were happy to be alive, but their lives would be changed forever. Over 300,000 were wounded. If they were lucky, they would only have a scar to remind them. Seventy-five thousand young men and women came home severely disabled ... for the rest of their lives. As we know today, though, some of those scars were in their hearts or part of their memory. Scars they couldn't see but that they have had to live with for the rest of their lives. And, Andy, GP has some of those scars."

Grandpa talked slowly, and his voice became strong again.

"Andy, when I hear a teacher teaching you about the Vietnam War and telling you things that were not true, it tells me a few things about the teacher. First, that teacher is not a veteran. Second, most likely none of his family, his parents, uncles, and aunts, ever served their country as part of our military. A veteran, even if not from the Vietnam War, would never say such things."

Grandpa went on to talk about the war. He said that people just don't understand what they are asking a soldier to do for them. It is not just placing them in harm's way. It's asking them to put their life on hold. To leave their children and family. They interrupt their education, their job or career, and everything that will be part of their future.

"The sad thing is that when they return home, they are different. Even if they did not see combat, the training itself conditioned them for combat. They learn to value the man beside them and to be willing to put their life on the line for their comrade. They learn that they must kill or be killed. They learn that the enemy doesn't even know you or your family, but he hates you and wants you dead. Can you imagine thinking that every moment of every day? Yet when you come home, you are expected to forget the war. Simply turn it off."

"Andy," Grandpa continued, "when we came home from Vietnam, we were not allowed to talk about our experiences. We couldn't share our feelings, sorrows, or even accomplishments with people. If people found out that I had served in Vietnam, they would denigrate me. Some would shout insults and admonishments for serving my and their country. And remember, Andy, they were the people who sent us to Vietnam. There are stories of Vietnam vets getting on to commercial airplanes and having the passengers boo them. They were advised not to wear their uniforms when traveling in public. What a disgrace.

"I was fortunate to have uncles who fought in WWII and Korea, who understood and would listen. Listen. Listen. They never judged. They knew and they shared some of their feelings ... not too different from mine. But you know, Andy, GP is proud of his service. I had some time when I was in harm's way but most of the time, I was either helping our soldiers or going out into the villages and hamlets to help the people who were intimidated and tortured by the enemy for supporting our soldiers.

Proud Moments That We Don't Talk About

"I remember the soldiers from the 82nd Airborne providing security so that I could get into a little hamlet and tend to the people ... yes, old men, women, and children. In one village, the enemy was in tunnels under the bombed-out building, while my team was on top, treating the wounded. When they were discovered, we were evacuated, and the 82nd guys took over."

"I still get emotional, Andy, not because of me, but because of what I saw. The tragic waste of life. I don't think any war is good, but it is part of survival on this earth. Wars have been fought for five thousand years. It doesn't make it right, but it's necessary for a survival.

"Was the war wrong? History will tell, but I think that the war was lost because of what was going on here in the States. When the politicians found it unpopular to prosecute the war, they abandoned our troops, the people of Vietnam, and allowed the communists to take over. We sent our troops to fight to preserve the democracy for the people of Vietnam. Eight million American men and women went because they were asked to go. Then we abandoned them and the people of Vietnam.

"If we take a lesson from that war, then we should never fight a war again. Get rid of the military and live happily ever after. But that's not reality. People always want what they have and what you have. We still have troops in Korea, Eastern Europe, the Middle East, Central America, and probably other places that we don't know about.

"So what do you do if called? You serve. But before that day comes, take responsibility for your country's actions and decisions. Make sure that you use your vote to elect people who will protect and preserve our democratic republic. We all have that responsibility. And if the time comes that it is necessary to fight to protect our country, then we all must step up and serve. Remember the priorities in our lives. Our God. Our Country.

Proud Moments That We Don't Talk About

Our Family."

"Grandpa, can I be a soldier?" Andy interrupted Grandpa.
"Of course you can, Andy." Grandpa smiled.
"Should all my friends be soldiers too?"

"Do you all say the Pledge of Allegiance each morning at school?"
Grandpa asked.
"Every morning, Grandpa."
"Next time, Andy, listen closely to the words. You will know
whether you should become a soldier."

"How do I become a soldier? Can my teacher make me a soldier?"
Andy asked.

"Not that Callahan guy who's teaching you all that stuff about
Vietnam. That's for sure," Grandpa said with emphasis. "Being
a soldier is an honor. You take on the responsibility of your
country. The people depend on you for their safety and security.
It is not a club that you can join. Some soldiers make the military
a career. Others, called the Reserves, serve when needed. All are
trained to be good soldiers."

"When you finish high school, you can make that decision. I'd
like to see you go to college and learn a skill or profession. Once
you have the skill, you can decide how you can use it to serve
your country. After high school, if you are not sure what you
want to do, joining the military can help you decide and focus.
I think everyone should have at least two years in the military
some time in their life. That might sound a bit scary, but the
military discipline is an important skill or attitude that can be
helpful throughout your life.

"Andy, don't worry about this now. I will guarantee you this. I
will be very proud of you when you wear the uniform. When I see
you, my chest will be so big, it will pop the buttons on my shirt.
For now, let's keep my buttons so Grandma doesn't have to fix

them." There was that twinkle in Grandpa's eye.

Grandpa's Notes

I pledge allegiance to the flag of the United States of America, and to the republic for which it stands, one nation, under God, indivisible, with liberty and justice for all.

I can't imagine why it is so difficult for some people to understand the pledge that they made so many times in school and in the public forum. Before we could openly say it, fifty-six men put their names and lives on the line. They signed the Declaration of Independence. If they were successful in their quest for independence from England, they would have created a new nation. If they were unsuccessful, they would be hanged for treason.

So how many men risked everything, life, limb, liberty, family, and possessions for this country? This country was built piece by piece with each sacrifice. Not just one, but many.

So how do I feel about the flag? The flag is just a piece of cloth. When I buy one, it is in a package, red, white, and blue with its dimensions and price sticker. The wrapper does not say how many stars and stripes, nor does it even give me a choice as to how many stars and stripes or a color preference. It is simply the American flag. If I want to display the America flag, this is it.

But the moment I take it out of the wrapper, it changes. I feel it. When I look at it, I want to hold it close to me. I remember as a little boy watching the parade and seeing Dad and the other men who were silently watching, then tipping their cap as the flag went by. I saluted but didn't know why. Maybe it was a man thing. Many of these men knew the pains of WWI and WWII. They stood, they tip their caps, and some just put their heads down. At one time, someone made the flag and put it in a wrapper to sell. Now it was on a flag pole, and it moved men's hearts.

The flag represents a country whose people will fight for the rights to life, liberty, and the pursuit of happiness. It tells the person who sees the flag that those who carry it believe in it and will fight for that which it stands.

So when I take the flag out of the wrapper and hang it in front of my house, it tells people what I stand for and will fight for, nothing less. I make sure the flag does not touch the ground. I make sure that a light shines on the flag at all times. When the flag becomes tattered, I see that it is discarded with honor. We don't throw the flag in the trash can.

So how can we permit a person in protest to step on the flag or burn the flag? We don't permit it. But they are only trashing a piece of colored cotton. Not the country for which it stands. Does it hurt to see someone try to disgrace the flag? Absolutely. But you will never see a veteran disgrace the flag. He knows what it stands for. To those who feel motivated to disgrace the flag in front of a veteran, the vet knows that they are cowards. The only good thing is that they are willing to declare their cowardice in public. They are the takers in our society. They will send your children to fight their battles. They never had a family member who served in the military. They don't know what's in the heart of a veteran.

A fellow, Dennis Ahola, told me of a firefight during the war. He said that they were getting overrun and the choppers were pulling them out. He was a gunner on the last chopper. As the last two soldiers were running toward the chopper, the last one saw that the flag was still in the camp. He ran back, grabbed it, and was running back to the chopper. As he fell to the ground, mortally wounded, his buddy jumped out of the chopper and grabbed the flag. Wounded, he reached the chopper as it lifted off. He threw the flag on to the chopper, and the gunner pulled him on board. He was dead. All for a piece of cloth? No. It was what it stood for. The enemy would have a trophy. Not a piece of cloth, but a trophy of what it stands for.

The flag is made up of thousands of stitches and many threads. It represents what we as a country stand for. It can only be taken apart a stitch or thread at a time. Just as many people do not know or understand all the sacrifices (stitches and threads) it took to make the flag, they also will not recognize when someone is taking it apart, a stitch at a time. All the stitches and threads make up the flag for which it stands.

So when we teach, "I pledge allegiance to the flag," it's not for a piece of cloth; it's "for which it stands, one nation, under God, indivisible, with liberty and justice for all."

A young man, George Vincent, a veteran from the 10th Mountain Division, USA, had an idea. He said that when we look at our society, it's not about what color we are, or where you or your family came from; it about where you are today. It's about red, white, and blue. He said that when you come to this country, you must assimilate in order to enjoy our freedoms. You must embrace our values and our system of justice. Otherwise, you are embracing someone else's values and system of justice. Most countries would call you the enemy. Can you imagine carrying the America flag in Nazi Germany during WWII or soviet Russia in the 1960s? George felt that we are all "red, white, and blue." What a great idea. Not new. That's what the first flag, thirteen stars, and thirteen stripes symbolized. His idea caught on, and now the flag logo is seen on clothing, cups, and hats in stores everywhere.

Thoughts on the Military

It would be nice not to have a military. Everyone could just get along. Just like in our families. Whoops! Not a good example. If two people can't get along, how can we expect five, ten, or thousands of people to get along? Wars have been fought for thousands of years. A strong military is necessary to keep the peace.

A strong military, which has been developed to support an aggressive ideology, may win a battle or war, but the ideology it supports will fail over time. An oppressed population will eventually rise up. It may take generations, but the ideology will succumb. When we look at history, wars have been fought for thousands of years. If the wars were so good, ultimately the succeeding ideology would prevail. But they don't prevail. They may surface again over generations, only to fail again. We need a strong military to support international law, to protect us, and to keep the peace. It's no different than our need for a strong civilian police force to maintain law and order and keep peace in our society. But serving in the military provides a generational benefit to our country. It teaches young men and women the importance of personal responsibility and accountability. It teaches comradery and the importance of being a part of something larger than one's self. When I was in high school, we had the draft. We just accepted the opportunity to serve our country. It was part of being a citizen in this country.

Some countries must conscript men in order to force them to fight at the whim of the dictator or king. They are soldiers in uniform but not soldiers at heart. They fight without a cause. Our soldiers fight for the needs of the people in their country. They know and believe in the cause. Our enemy knows how our soldiers think. They bomb civilians to scare the people and use people for protection when they are scared. Our soldiers protect the people, often at the expense of their own safety. And they would do it again. My teams did it in Vietnam.

What Can We Do?

Our children should be taught about wars, the good and the bad. The more we understand the process, the more likely we will recognize potential enemies. If understanding does not prevent a war, it will at least help us understand the enemy and shorten the war.

These are my thoughts on the military. There has been a whole generation since the draft who never received the benefit of the military training. Now, all of our military are volunteers. They volunteered to serve their country. Our country benefits not only from the best trained military but from young men and women who will be leaders and teachers to the next generation.

What is exciting today is that there is a whole generation of young brains who are comfortable with sophisticated technology. They play games on their computers and smart phones. They interact with players all over the world. Today, young people play games, but those skills, strategy, and hand-eye coordination will help them fly airplanes in the future while sitting in front of a computer screen thousands of miles away. These are the warriors of the future. We need to give them the tools and the history of warfare to help them use their talents when we need them.

Ask a Vet

Vets don't complain. They just do what needs to be done. Vets don't complain. They see the big picture.

People fight battles. Vets fight wars.
People think for the todays. Vets think for future generations.

When will all the wars end? When there are no longer any more people. The last two people on earth probably will still complain about something until they hit each other with a club or die from a toothache.

The people who cause the war may only feel discomfort or inconvenience for their action. People who fight the war feel the pain for a moment. Then they die. The people who survive the war live with the pain for generations.

A few weeks went by after the garden talk. Grandpa and Andy were sitting on the bench in the garden. Andy told Grandpa that he talked to his teacher and told him what he had said.

Grandpa looked at Andy. "Probably not the best thing to do, Andy. Some of those teachers don't take kindly to someone telling them what to teach."

"My teacher said he wants to meet you. He said he thinks you and he should talk."

"That's fine with me, Andy, but he probably won't like what I have to say," Grandpa replied. "He comes from a whole different generation. They just don't understand guys like me."

Mr. Callahan called Grandpa, and they set up a meeting. He agreed to meet Grandpa at the house. Grandpa thought that he would be on home turf and they could at least sit out in the garden.

Proud Moments That We Don't Talk About

Teacher Calls on Grandpa

Mr. Callahan surprised Grandpa. He was dressed neatly. He had close-cropped, neat, early graying hair. He was not covered with tattoos, and there wasn't any metal hanging from his ears. He was polite and respectful. As they walked down toward the garden, he listened to Grandpa describe his flowerbeds. Mr. Callahan actually knew a little about flowers. He grew many of the same flowers that Grandpa had, but he quietly listened. Grandpa seemed to be doing all the talking.

Finally, Grandpa stopped and turned. "Mr. Callahan, Andy said that you and I need to talk. What's on your mind? Apparently, we have some different opinions about the Vietnam War. What do you know about that war? It was thirty years ago."

Mr. Callahan just looked at Grandpa. He thought, "Was this old guy looking for a fight?" He reached out his hand, took Grandpa's hand, and said, "Thank you for your service, sir. I know you did not hear that very often when you came home."

Grandpa just froze. Only recently had he heard anyone thank a vet for his service.

Mr. Callahan went on. "Grandpa, I hate teaching about the Vietnam War. I know that we are not teaching the truth about that war. We are teaching what the politicians want us to teach, not what our soldiers saw and experienced. There weren't any baby killers. They didn't kill civilians. Our soldiers risked their lives and saved civilians. Grandpa, I know about the war. I lived it."

Mr. Callahan became intense. "Grandpa, my father was killed in Vietnam in 1968. He was a pilot and was shot down in the Mekong Delta. He piloted a small plane called a FAC that went out and spotted the enemy. They told my mom that when they found him, he was severely wounded and that people had taken his clothes."

Grandpa didn't say a word. He just sat there. He thought, "This sounds so familiar." It was a flashback.

Grandpa recalled an incident when he was in the Mekong Delta. He headed a team that would go out in the villages and hamlets to tend to the sick and wounded. The facilities were primitive, makeshift at best. He was in an open marketplace in the middle of a little village. Ducks, fish, unknown meats hung from the rafters. Tables that were piled high with vegetables and wares for sale by local vendors surrounded them.

This was the first mission in a few days. The people had been requesting our help. Two days before, we aborted the mission when one of our FAC (forward air control) planes went down nearby. They found the pilot about a kilometer away from his plane. He was badly injured. He did not make it back to the base. When they found him, all his gear, radio, emergency kit, and even his uniform and shoes were gone.

The enemy got to him first.

Grandpa recalls that for security reasons, they set up in the middle of the market. The thinking was that if "Charlie" was around, he would not try anything that could hurt the people in the village. Security was tight. Our soldiers, 82nd Airborne, were all around us. Just watching. Just looking for any clues.

Grandpa had seen several patients, and more people were crowding into the treatment area. Some needed help, some wanted our handouts, and some were just curious. As Grandpa was tending to a little boy with an infection, he heard someone shouting behind him. He couldn't understand, but when he looked up, the people and the little boy had panic on their faces. Grandpa turned around and looked into the barrel of a pistol.

Grandpa remembered the incident as if it was yesterday. The man holding the pistol was wearing a US Air force flight suit and was shouting at Grandpa. The man looked at Grandpa. His face was red. The neck veins were distended. Panic. At any minute something was going to happen. Looking at the end of the barrel inches from his face, he could only see the faces of his wife, Ida, and little Andrea and Audrey in flashes. What would they do without him?

Grandpa couldn't understand a word. The man shouted louder and louder. He turned back to Grandpa and then back again toward the soldiers. The soldiers were slowly coming toward him. If they open fire, they would also hit Grandpa and some of the people. The people were running for cover. Grandpa had choices. Attack, distract, or retract. He knew he could not get his weapon fast enough to attack. The pistol was at his forehead. Distract may give soldiers a better shot. Retract probably would only mean a shot in the back of the head.

As the man turned back and forth, Grandpa took a step back. When the man turned back toward Grandpa, he would step forward and push the pistol at Grandpa's head. A few steps. A few steps. Grandpa's back was against a post. When the man turned away from Grandpa, Grandpa dropped down, spun around the post, and pulled his weapon. By the time Grandpa pulled his weapon, shots were fired. Smoke and dust everywhere. People screaming. The man slumped to the ground. Grandpa was clear. The soldiers did their job.

The soldiers called in support to get Grandpa and his team out of there. The soldiers had more work to do. When Grandpa got back to the base, they told him that the man with the pistol was wearing the downed pilot's flight suit. When they saw him, he ran into the marketplace for cover. They said that when they surrounded the market, he decided to use Grandpa's Medcap team for protection. Bad choice.

Proud Moments That We Don't Talk About

That night, Grandpa got the shakes. His hand trembled as he wrote his nightly letter to his Ida. He just broke down. He almost lost them all.

Grandpa looked over to Mr. Callahan. He had tears streaming down his face. "You can be very proud of your dad. And, Mr. Callahan, can I call you Andy?"

"Sure," Mr. Callahan replied.

"Andy, your father would be very proud of you. I want you to make sure that your mom also knows about our visit. She should meet my wife, Ida."

Mr. Callahan still did not know what was happening. All he said to Grandpa was that his dad was a FAC pilot and was killed in Vietnam. But Grandpa knew more of the story. He and Andy sat for several hours. Grandpa told Andy about the experience he had had in the village in the Mekong Delta. Andy just listened. Thirty years later, Grandpa met that pilot's son. It was Andy's teacher, Andy Callahan.

Chapter 4

Kiss It Up: The Five-Second Rule

Andy came back to the table and sat down across from Grandpa.

"I've often wondered, Grandpa, why they have to have a sign up in the restroom to tell the employees to wash their hands before they go back to work. Don't they know that they're supposed to wash their hands after they go to the bathroom?"

Grandpa looked up and smiled. "Andy, there are two reasons why the sign is up there. The most logical reason is to remind the employees that, for their own health, it is important to wash their hands before touching food or touching anything else. E. coli is a common bacteria that is found in a bathroom and which, if it contaminates food, can cause very serious infections. You would expect an individual in their day-to-day activities outside of their workplace to know that they should wash their hands every time they use the bathroom. But some children are not taught personal hygiene and cleanliness by their parents, and the school system does not address personal hygiene until they are teenagers.

"The second reason why that sign is up is to protect the restaurant owner. If there is an E. coli outbreak in his restaurant and it is attributed to unhygienic practices by the employees, the owner can simply say, 'I put a sign up to remind them to wash their hands before coming back to work.' We expect the employees who handle our food to practice good personal hygiene. Unfortunately, we can't have 'hand-washing inspectors' in our restrooms."

Kiss It Up: The Five-Second Rule

"When Grandma and Grandpa were growing up, we were taught to wash our hands, not only when we used the restroom, but especially before we sat down to eat. We grew up in a time when the doctors did not always know what caused infections. More importantly, they did not have many successful ways to manage or treat infections. Something as simple as an infected tooth could cause an infection that can rapidly spread to the neck and throat and ultimately cause death. Today we know what causes infections, how the body fights infections, and we have drugs that can help the body fight the infection.

"When we were growing up, if we dropped a piece of food or candy that we really wanted, we would quickly reach down and pick it up and say, 'Kiss it up.' We were kissing it up to

God in hopes that if we ate this food on the floor, we would not get sick. It sounds silly today, but we were taught that we could not eat anything that fell on the floor without first washing or cleaning it.

"Today, 'kissing it up' is not good enough. We have a better understanding of the causes of infection and how infections can be spread. There are many examples in history, Andy, how infections spread and killed millions of people. The plague killed one-third of the population of Europe in the 1300s and spread from rats to fleas to humans. Most people who were infected died. Six hundred years later, antibiotics were discovered and the disease was nearly eradicated.

"Tuberculosis, called consumption, killed millions with a slow death of suffocation. It was spread by saliva from spitting or sneezing and was nearly eradicated with the discovery of antibiotics. Smallpox, recorded in ancient times, was brought to America from Europe and Asia. It ravaged the Native American population. Touching the infected areas on the skin spread the disease. It was eradicated in the 1970s with vaccinations."

Grandpa explained that, over time, we have learned how to treat these infections and, probably most important, how to prevent them. But we still have a large population, even in our sophisticated society, who do not understand how infections spread among the people.

Picking a Paddy

"Let me give you an example of how an infection might spread. One day, you saw a cow paddy in the pasture and didn't know what it was. You pick it up, look at it, and then decide because it didn't really smell that good, you threw it back down in the pasture. On the way home, you saw an apple hanging from the tree, so you pick the apple. You took your penknife out of your pocket and sliced the apple. You started enjoying that nice sweet flavor. When you got home, you told Mom about the apple. Then you sat down and made yourself a nice sandwich. You got out your favorite lunchmeat and placed two pieces on a thick slice of bread. You picked up one piece of meat and just rolled it up and ate it without any bread. Back to the refrigerator to get a can of pop and then you sat down to enjoy that delicious sandwich."

"I don't see any problem with making my own sandwich, Grandpa. I do it all the time," Andy questioned Grandpa.

"Now this is the big question, Andy. Would you be willing to take a piece of that cow pie that you found in the pasture and lay it on your sandwich before you took a bite? My bet is you would say, 'Absolutely not.'"

"No way, Grandpa. That would be foolish. Yuck!" Andy replied.

Grandpa continued, "If I told you, yet that's exactly what you did, would you deny it?"

"Of course, Grandpa. You know I would never eat a cow pie."

Grandpa smiled. "You would say that you did not bring the cow pie home with you. You knew that it smelled terrible, so you threw it back in the pasture. Now let's take a look at the tiny amounts of bacteria that are in that cow paddy and let's see what happened to them.

"When you picked up the paddy, some of bacteria got on your fingers. It stayed on your fingers as you walked toward the apple tree. When you picked the apple, some of the bacteria transferred from your fingers to the apple. You reached in your pocket to get your penknife, some of the bacteria stayed on the cloth in your pocket but also on your penknife. When you sliced the apple, you took some of the bacteria that was on the skin of the apple plus the bacteria on the knife and drove the bacteria down into each slice of the apple. How are you feeling so far?"

Andy just stared at Grandpa. He thought, "What is Grandpa up to?"

"Now you ate the apple, and the bacteria that made up the cow paddy, and you know where that came from, is now in your mouth. But the apple tasted so good. As you walked home and anxious to tell everyone about the apple that you found, you touched the doorknob with the fingers that picked up the paddy. You put your hands on the counter with the same fingers, opened up the refrigerator, hands on the refrigerator handle, and made yourself a nice sandwich with the fingers that picked up the paddy in the pasture.

"You picked up the meat for your sandwich with those same fingers and even put one piece of the meat in your mouth with those same fingers. You made the sandwich, ate the sandwich, and drank the pop with the same fingers that picked up the paddy that was deposited by the cow in the pasture. How's it going so far, Andy?" Grandpa asked.

Andy just sat there, listening to the story.

Our Defense System

"At this point, your body has some work to do. Any of the bacteria from the paddy must be destroyed. Our body has a tremendous defense system to fight infections. If the bacteria from the paddy are confined to our digestive tract, then it likely will not be a problem. But suppose, you had a little cut on your finger, the bacteria from the paddy could cause a very serious infection. Suppose, you touched your face or, worse, your eye, the bacteria could cause an even more serious infection.

"The bacteria from the paddy can also be spread to other people. When you put your fingers on the refrigerator handle, the bacteria was deposited on the handle. Anyone touching the handle afterward has the bacteria on their hands. And what about the friend that you met on the way home? Did you shake hands with him? Does he have the bacteria from the paddy on his hands? Yes!

"Andy, the example of this paddy may sound extreme, but it does show how something as simple as picking up a paddy can actually spread an infection. So how could this chain of infection be broken? When you picked up the paddy and determined that it was bad, simply washing your hands and washing the bacteria off your hand would have broken the whole chain. You could've cut the apple, eaten the apple, shook hands with your friend, touched the front door handle, touched the refrigerator handle, and even eaten the whole sandwich without any worry of the bacteria from the paddy in the pasture."

Andy was starting to feel a little sick.

The Binh Thuy Crapper

In poor countries around the world, one of the major causes of death is the result of water contamination. Cholera is the main disease that we see as a result of water contamination. Grandpa told the story of when he was in Vietnam and of the famous Binh Thuy Crapper. As he and his medical team would make their way to the hospital, they would cross a bridge over one of the canals. At the edge of the canal was a platform with a two-seater outhouse. Everything from the outhouse dropped down into the canal. Children were swimming under and downstream from the Binh Thuy Crapper while the women washed clothes further downstream. Further downstream were people with buckets and bottles gathering water to take back to their houses in the village. Not only was the water contaminated from the Binh Thuy Crapper, but they contaminated their skin, their clothes, and the food that they ate.

One of the missions that Grandpa and his team focused on was water purification. Something as simple as drinking, washing, and swimming upstream from where you were pooping could save lives. It was sometimes hard to sell that message to the people because they could not see the bacteria and they could not make the connection between bacteria and the diseases from which they suffered.

Fifty Years Later

Fifty years later, we still have that same problem in many parts of the world. Fifty years later, we still have people in our own country who don't understand the relationship between bacteria and disease. That's why we have to have signs in the restrooms. Simply breaking the chain of contamination can prevent most bacterial diseases. When we didn't understand diseases as we do today, we would drink spring water, well water, or upstream river water. We learned to wash our foods and wash our hands. We couldn't see the bacteria, but we knew that it was important to wash our hands and food before eating. I wonder if we have just forgotten to teach our children to wash before eating and wash when they use the bathroom.

Don't Kiss It Up ... Pick It Up

A while back, Grandma and I were at a restaurant, and when the waitress came over to take our order, she noticed the creamer on the floor beside our table. She politely picked it up and put it on our table. I was amazed that she did not even think twice about at least saying, "Kiss it up," before putting the creamer on our table. She never heard of the "five-second rule."

Kiss It Up: The Five-Second Rule

Five-Second Rule:
If you pick it up within five seconds, dirt, bugs, and bacteria don't have a chance to get on board. Absolutely no scientific proof that it works, but it keeps you from throwing out a perfectly good piece of candy.

When I asked her why she put the dirty creamer on our table, she looked at me with surprise. When I explained that it was on the floor and that because it was on the floor, she should not have put it on the table. She still seemed surprised. When I explained to her that people walk on the floor and that by putting the creamer on my table, it was the same as people walking on the table, she still did not get it. She was surprised when I told her that people walk from the parking lot into the restaurant and whatever is on their shoes in the parking lot is now on the floor of the restaurant. She seemed amazed at this discovery.

I was having difficulty trying to be polite and not show my frustration with the stupidity of this server. I finally decided to simplify things and asked, "If you were eating and accidentally dropped your fork on the floor, would you pick it up and use it or ask for a new fork?" She looked at me, thought a while, and then said, "Ask for a new fork?" She was hoping she gave me the right answer, but she wasn't sure.

She turned away, and a few minutes later a new waiter came to our table. It was obvious that the young lady was upset with me. More disturbing was the fact that the young lady did not know that you do not pick up things off the floor and put them on the eating table—especially in front of your customer. Just think what goes on behind the scenes.

It's bad enough that they don't know about contamination of food, but it's worse they don't even know to say, "Kiss it up," before they pick it up. (That could be the name of a song sung in the kitchens of restaurants all over the country.) So now we know why they have to have signs in the restrooms telling employees to wash their hands before they go back to work. There are actually people who do not know that if they happen to pick up a paddy in the pasture, they should not taste it. And they should wash their hands before they eat their next sandwich.

Breaking the Chain

The key to fighting infections is to focus on preventing infection. Prevention means we must break the chain between the source and host of the infection. We focus on killing rats and fleas to stop the plague. We focus on purifying water to prevent cholera. We vaccinate our children to eradicate smallpox. And we break the contagious chain of tuberculosis by controlling exposure to the saliva of infected people.

The firemen will tell you that they spend more time working to prevent fires than on fighting fires. Prevention can prevent hundreds of fires from starting, but once a fire starts, success depends on the available resources. Are there enough firemen? Is there enough water? They can only fight one fire at a time.

When it comes to managing infectious disease, efforts in prevention can help millions, while treatment is limited to available resources. Are there enough doctors? Is there enough medicine?

Breaking the chain, cutting the cause-and-effect link is not that easy. The common denominator in all the prevention efforts is the host, the patient. It's people who smoke when they know smoking is related to respiratory disease and cancer. It's people who poop upstream and drink downstream. It's people who expose themselves to communicable disease. And in 99 percent of cases, kissing it up won't help.

Grandpa's Notes

Clean versus Sterility

I arrived at Can Tho Hospital to see civilian patients who had been caught in the war. The VC had little compassion for the civilians. They went into the villages, took what they needed, and punished anyone who resisted. Most of the wounds were cuts and blunt trauma. These required debridement and repair (suture or wires).

It is interesting that many of these wounds were dirty and often infected. Most of the wounds were two or three days to as much as a week old. Family members carried the patients or brought them on bicycles, carts, or little trucks to the hospital. You would think that these patients would be in a lot of pain, but they didn't show or exhibit symptoms of severe pain. When we manipulated the wounds while doing the examination, the patients sat or laid there quietly.

Even though my area of interest and responsibility involved facial wounds, I do not remember the general surgeon that I worked with having to do many amputations. In some cases, wounds were so severe that a decision had to be made, "Do we let this patient sit and see if he will live while we operate on other patients that we know will survive?" Those were tough and eye-opening decisions for me. Life, at this time, had not prepared me for making life-and-death decisions.

I was thrown into this environment because I had more surgery training than any of the other docs at the base. That did not make me qualified to do major facial surgery as I learned years later, but what I knew at the time helped the people the best way that we could. The general surgeon, who was from another base, coached me through some of the trauma cases, but he was also not trained in facial trauma. As it turned out, he and I were in the same situation. He had some general surgery training but was not a trauma surgeon.

Could we have done more for our patients?

If we had had major trauma training, we would have had more experience at our disposal, but could we have executed the experience in the environment in which we had to work? For optimum care for the patient, the surgeon needs knowledge, skill, experience, and most important, an environment to execute his skills. What kind of environment did we have in Can Tho?

The Environment: Clean but Not Sterile

The operating suite had two operating rooms with open holes in the wall where there used to be windows. Birds could fly in and out or perch on the IV poles. I remember a chicken sitting on the windowsill, just enjoying the scene. The techs didn't think anything of it. They just let him enjoy the operation. What about sterility? Really?

We draped the patient with whatever we had available. I never questioned where the drapes came from or whether they had been washed. Could have been downstream from the Binh Thuy Crapper. I wore my jungle fatigues and then changed to whatever surgical gowns were available. Sometimes I wore my full uniform, sometimes a scrub top, and rarely a complete surgical scrub gown. Our instruments were sterilized, but once they were opened, touched, moved around the OR, I assumed they were clean, not sterile. We used a lot of alcohol and soap to wipe instruments when we thought they might be contaminated.

Betadine (iodine solution) and Ivory soap were used to clean the patients. But what about the water? We used lots of water and hoped it was not from the Mekong River. We had sterile water for flushing wounds, but that was not always available.

Before I started to repair a facial wound, I checked to see what supplies were available. Suture varied from cardiac suture to fine plastic surgery suture. We worked with what we had at the time. Using large suture to repair fine wounds left more scarring. Large wounds repaired with fine suture broke down after a few days. We worked with what we had at the time. Since we had limited follow-up with our patients, some deeper wounds we left open to heal from the inside out. This is how deep wounds were treated years ago before the use of antibiotics or antiseptic solutions.

The patient was brought by his family from the hospital ward to the OR building. They crossed a bare dirt courtyard with clouds of dust from all the people walking around. They wheeled the patient to the door and knocked. We opened the door, wheeled him in, and closed the door. The family sat outside until we finished.

When we finished the operation, we pushed the patient out the door to the family. They took the patient across the courtyard and back to the ward. The wards were long rooms with rows of beds. Two or three patients were assigned to each bed. Two patients sat up while one laid down. They simply took turns. The family sat around on the floor at the foot and between the beds.

For security reasons, we could not leave the operating room building and go out into the courtyard until the courtyard was cleared. This meant that when I arrived in the morning, I would have to stay there until we finished operating. I had to be off the roads and back at my base before six o'clock. The roads were not considered secure after 6:00 p.m.

So after surgery, the courtyard was cleared, and our team would go to the ward to review our patients and write orders. The Vietnamese nurses were very helpful and determined to take good care of the patients. The sad problem was that there were so many patients and very limited personnel and supplies.

So how did we do it?

This was 1968, and medicine had made a lot of strides in order to save people's lives. But we had to work as if this was 1944 and World War II, or even World War I, or the Civil War. During the Civil War, minor perforation wounds of the abdomen resulted in infections and subsequently killed the patient. It was not the wound itself but the bacteria that was released from the perforation of the gut that caused the infection and death. A wound to the arm or leg often required amputation to prevent the spread of gangrene. World War II wounds had similar challenges. We had better knowledge of the infection process but were limited in treatment options.

But this was 1968. Why the same challenges? It was not what we knew; it was the environment in which we were working. In 1988, I worked with the International Medical Corp in Honduras. We were helping the contra freedom fighters. The conditions were better, only to the extent that we had more and better supplies. We were much closer to a sterile operating field.

These wounds were different from the Vietnam civilian

wounds. These wounds were mostly severe facial gunshot wounds. Pieces or parts of the face were missing or destroyed. The interesting twist from 1968 was that the wounded soldier had to "walk" from the battlefield in Nicaragua and cross the Coco River in order to reach our field hospital. If he survived the evacuation, he had a good chance of surviving his wounds. Soldiers who sustained a puncture wound of the abdomen or chest wall developed severe infections by the time they got to us or died along the way. Soldiers with leg and arm wounds often cut away the tissue as it turned gray or black. This prevented the spread of gangrene, saved their life, but cost them an extremity. To the soldier, it meant survival. Where did he learn this? How could he cut off his own toe, foot, or leg? And just a little bit at a time.

What I Learned

The body fights to stay alive—in spite of what we do personally to shut it down. The body has so many defense mechanisms to keep it working. Sometimes, I think the brain, which runs the controls to keep us alive, puts us in the very environment that overrides all the body's defenses and ultimately shuts it down. The brain told me to jump off the garage roof when I was only nine years old. "Superman can fly, so why can't I?" was the brain's logic. The parts of my body that had to spend the next eight weeks repairing the broken leg wondered whether we might need a new brain.

The practice of medicine deals with helping the body repair broken parts and systems. Many of the medical issues that we deal with are the result of conscious decisions. Not all, but many. I was told that our body was built to last 145 years. Just like the car that should last 250,000 miles, it doesn't, and we don't. If we disregard proper maintenance and safe driving skills, we accept, by default, that our car will not last the 250,000 miles. Similarly, if we disregard healthy and safe lifestyle choices, we, by default, accept that we will not make our 145th birthday.

I have learned that as a surgeon, I can only help the body survive. The operative word is *help*. I cannot make it survive. If I put the broken parts together, we have to wait for the body system to make them functional. The body repairs a cut by activating a system that removes damaged tissue and replaces it with new skin. We only see a red line, a little swelling, and then a scab. When the scab falls off, it's healed. If we interfere with the healing process or if there is loss of tissue, then there is a scar, a reminder not to do it again. Even if the cut required stitches, the repair process still must occur. The surgeon can only help the process; he did not make it happen. We can transplant a kidney, but the body must accept it and put it into function.

Once I realized that I could only facilitate the healing process, my mission changed. I became comfortable with doing the best that I could in any environment with the tools that were available. In Vietnam, we cleaned, removed dead tissue, and put things back together to facilitate the healing process. If the patients couldn't keep it clean, then the wounds most likely got infected. We did the best that we could do.

In the jungles of Honduras, the first question I asked was, "How much fuel do we have for the generators?" The fuel determined how long the generators would run and thus how much time we had to operate. We had to decide to do ten short operations or one long operation. Tough decisions. A patient's life or deformity might depend on a fifty-five-gallon drum of diesel fuel. Sad. Tough. But true.

The operative phrase is "helping the body do what it can and is supposed to do." You can't force the body to repair a system or broken part. We can't make a baby walk. We can help him stand, teach him to walk, and catch him when he falls. We can't make a person get well, but we can help him. If he keeps doing the same thing over and over, then it's not the body, it is the brain that needs the help—and that's the hard one.

Convincing thirsty people not to drink contaminated water, an alcoholic to stop drinking, or a man smoking through his tracheostomy to quit smoking is almost impossible. It's the brain that is overriding facts and good sense. But that is the life lesson. We can only help; we cannot force. We can help them achieve success; we can't make them successful. Help the people who want to be helped, and don't worry about the people who don't want to be helped. You will ultimately help more people with less frustration.

"You can't teach a pig to sing. It frustrates you and aggravates the pig."

Just a Thought

Our body takes oxygen from the atmosphere and distributes it to the cells that in turn release carbon dioxide to the atmosphere. The CO_2 is used by plants along with sunlight to grow and release oxygen back into the atmosphere for our body to use. It is a nice practical million-year relationship. The body also needs fuel for the cellular combustion in its cells. Plants and other organisms provide that fuel.

If we have all the oxygen and fuel we need, why don't we live forever? God only knows.

D.Mata 2014

Chapter 5

Growth Is a Decision

Trying New Things: When Fearless Meets Dumb

Andy enjoyed listening to GP. Sometimes a simple question would bring on a whole lecture. GP had a little twinkle in his eye when he was on a roll. He seemed to always have a point to be made, but the route to the point could take several turns.

GP liked to ask questions during his talks to make you think. It seemed that GP was not always looking for a right answer.

He just wanted you to think about the question. It was the process that was important. Andy found that he used that same technique as he interacted with classmates. GP said that if you wanted to know what 2 + 2 equals, there are two things that you can learn from the question. You can learn that the answer is 4. But learning why 2 + 2 = 4, learning to add, would be the more valuable answer.

One of GP's favorite challenges to Andy and the kids was to try new things. He said that your growth depends on trying new things. The more you learn, the more you grow. Success depends on learning new things. Success depends on continuing to grow, being willing to try new things. Being willing to change. That's the growth process.

If success depends on growth—learning and trying new things— why do some people refuse to try new things? Why do some people quit learning? Some people quit learning because they think they know. All the kids could recite the Grandpa saying:

> When you think you know, you probably don't.
> When you think you know everything, you don't.
> When you know that you know everything, it's time
> to sit down, shut up, and listen.

Andy remembered GP telling stories about pounding nails, eating baluts and turtle eggs, and seeing his first wounded soldiers. Some stories were about trying new things and others were about having new things put before him. Either way, GP said he had to make a decision to learn from them. He used the experience as a foundation for things to come. Some he looked forward to, and some he feared.

I'm Not Good at Golf

Andy and GP were at lunch one day. Andy's friend Michael came over to their table. "What are you guys up to today?" he asked.

"GP and I are going to the driving range to hit balls," Andy replied. "Want to come join us?"

"No, thanks. I'm not really good at golf," Michael replied. GP looked up and smiled. "Where have you golfed before?"

"I've never golfed, but I know that I'm not good at it," Michael said.

GP restrained himself. "Well, if you ever want to learn, let Andy know and we can go to the range together."

After Michael left the table, Andy looked at GP. "How does he know that he is not good at golf if he never tried it before? Why doesn't he just try it first?"

Andy remembered that time in the restaurant. GP told him that there are several reasons that could be keeping Michael from learning to golf. GP said it could be something as simple as no one has ever offered to teach him. He just doesn't know how much fun he could be missing. He could be embarrassed because Andy already knows how to golf. He could be afraid to try something new, afraid to fail.

Fearlessness versus Stupidity

One thing for sure, GP wasn't afraid of trying new things. He remembered GP telling the story about hanging from an H-53 rescue helicopter over the Mekong River and another about testing the effects of mountain currents in a Cessna 172 airplane. GP would deny he was fearless. He would claim that sometimes fearless bordered on dumb.

One day, Andy's cousin Mark asked GP to go for a ride on his bike. GP was in his seventies, but "once you know how to ride a bike, you never forget." Mark said that all he could remember was GP asking, "What's this for?" over and over. "What do you need all these gadgets for? When I was a kid, all we needed was two wheels, two pedals, and a seat."

GP's famous wisdom was being tested. "When you know you know everything, it's time to sit down, shut up, and listen." Mark said he felt bad for GP and was a bit concerned that GP might have difficulty mastering all the "newfangled stuff" on the bike.

They were about three miles out on the bike trail when GP declared his independence. Mark was about one hundred yards ahead on the trail. He remember hearing, "Hey, Mark, no hands," and then the crash. By the time Mark turned around, GP was getting up and assuring him that he was OK. GP forgot that when you take your hands off the brakes, you can't stop.

"These newfangled bikes. Who puts the brakes on the handlebars?" GP had a few scrapes and bruises. Mark felt bad, not so much about the scrapes, but because of GP's pride. GP was OK with the whole incident. He said it was a moment when fearless and dumb overlapped.

Andy thought about GP and how he talked about why people try and don't try new things. Andy wondered why some people just don't try.

Same ole! Same ole!
Doing the same thing over and over but expecting different results.

Grandpa's Notes

We learn from information that is put before us, either intentionally or unintentionally. We have little control over the unintentional. If you trip and fall, it is a learning experience. You generally don't look for an opportunity to fall. Failing at something is unintentional but can be a learning experience. Failing is a learning experience so long as we don't quit. You are not a failure unless you quit. *The most successful people are the people who failed the most but never quit.*

Intentional learning means putting ourselves in a learning environment. We choose to sit in a class and listen to someone whose knowledge or wisdom we respect. We try new things to challenge our thinking and to build on what we already know. Unintentional learning is like putting the pieces of a puzzle together without having the picture in front of you. The only thing you know is that there is a piece somewhere that will fit and will complete the picture. The picture might be a goal or dream that we wish to accomplish. The final picture might be the picture of our life. (*Be careful not to pick up the final piece too soon.*)

> *Common sense is not so common.*
> —*Voltaire*

Common Sense: Why Not Use It?

Common sense is the common denominator of our existence. Things that are obvious and support survival make up our common sense. Common sense is the foundation on which we make our decisions. We start the decision process with common sense and then enhance it with additional facts. The facts (knowledge) come from our own experiences and what we have learned from others.

We often judge the outcome of an action based on common sense first and then on additional understanding (facts) of the event.

Growth Is a Decision

Information	Event	Action
Common sense.	Don't step out into traffic.	Safe decision.
Common sense + facts.	But a child is stepping into traffic.	Heroic decision.
Common sense + facts.	But a dollar bill is on the street.	Fatal decision.

We use common sense in the decision to react or respond. If we are in the reaction mode, then common sense has a higher priority. Save the child at the expense of our own safely. If we are in the response mode, then we apply more facts (knowledge) to the action decision. Try to stop the traffic and save you and the child.

But sometimes, decisions based on common sense have an untoward outcome. The result of the decision, good or bad, still becomes part of our own experience or reference. Good or bad, we make the decision. How we apply common sense to the decision-making process affects whether we move on or stay put.

So why do some people go throughout their lives focusing on the future and moving forward while others live in the past, not even trying to move forward? We all have common sense, but we have different motivations. If the common denominator is common sense, then knowledge is the variable that differentiates us. As knowledge increases, we decrease the value (priority) of common sense. The more we learn, the more we grow. We can't stand still and grow. Growth implies moving on. What are some of the elements that affect our decision to stay put or move on?

Move On or Stay Put: The Elements of Movement

There are six main elements that influence our decision to stay put or move on.

1. Fear of the unknown.
2. Self-esteem. What will other people think?
3. Value of the event. No perceived value—pleasure, reward.
4. Risk to benefit.
5. Morality. Right versus wrong.
6. Priority. How does it fit in my life plan?

We can overcome our fears with the knowledge and understanding of the events and circumstances that currently justify our fears.

Fear: False Evidence Appearing Real

How can we be afraid of something that we have never experienced? Conversely, do we have to try something in order to be afraid or respect the danger? Fear is a learned attitude. We are not born afraid of flying, afraid of heights, or afraid of going to the dentist. Fear is a learned response to information from our environment. Good information, either from personal experience or the experience of others, will be the basis for our fear. We can overcome any fear with additional information. If we learned to be afraid, then we can learn *not* to be afraid. It takes a decision, a willingness to seek information and understanding.

When I hear someone say, "But you don't understand my circumstances" I think I probably do. After all, my circumstances cause me to eat the turtle eggs.

More often than not, our fears are perceptions rather than predictions of the future.

Fear is based on our perception of the action or event before us. We overcome our fears with knowledge and understanding of the events and circumstances that currently justify our fears. Most fears are founded in the unknown. We don't know all the elements of the event. Therefore, we hypothesize. We guess at what might happen if we proceed. We can fear for our safety or our health. We can fear what we think other people might say. But more often than not, our fears are perceptions rather than predictions of the future.

"Can Do" and "Can't Do" People

Can do people are our cheerleaders. They want us to succeed. Can't do people keep us where they are comfortable with us. They create boundaries to impede our success. We justify our fears based on the information that we have at the moment. If we are surrounded by "can't do" people, then we justify our fears based on their attitudes. If we are surrounded by "can do" people, our cheerleaders, we are able to reject fear with a "can do" success attitude. Keep in mind that information is only as good as the credibility of the source (see chapter 11, "The Cycle of Influence").

Move On or Stay Put: Dealing with Fears

We deal with fear of the unknown every day in our lives. The decision to move on or stay put is a process. We consider everything that we have learned coupled with good old common sense, and we make the decision. We process the fear with knowledge and understanding.

Fear Can Paralyze

Why do people say that they are not good at something when they have never even tried it? It's OK to be bad at something. Just try (see chapter 7, "It's OK to Be Bad"). It is interesting to hear the reasons why people will not try something new or different. Common sense, motivation, and priorities are the factors that move us from "don't try" to "try, at least once."

Common sense is an important and natural consideration. There are times, however, when we are forced to try new things. I do not have to fall off the roof a couple of times to prove that I am really not good at walking on a steep roof. However, I do not have to practice walking on a steep roof, and get good at it, before I go out on the roof for safety when the building is on fire.

Primary fear: The building is on fire and I will be burned.
Common sense: Run through the fire or away from the fire.
Motivation: I don't want to get burned.
Priority: I have one minute to make up my mind and get out on the roof.
New fear: I'm not good at walking on roof. What if I fall off the roof?
Choice: Burn for sure or possibly fall off the roof.

Sadly, some people will let the fear of failure paralyze them. They perish in their anxiety and fear. We hear stories of people who are so afraid of grabbing the rescuer's hand and stepping out on the ladder only to go back into the building and perish.

Growth Is a Decision

Fears are perceptions rather than predictions of the future.

Fear	Decision	Information	Decision
Killed in crash	Won't fly	Flying is safe.	Buy ticket
Killed in wreck	Don't drive	Need to go to work	Learn to drive
Dentist	Refuse care	Pain in tooth	It's not that bad.
Needles	Refuse shot	May save your life	It's worth the pinch.
Heights	Avoid windows	I don't care.	Dirty windows
Public speaking	Don't speak up	I have a message.	Speak up.

Move On or Stay Put: Value of the Event

We will move on or stay put, try something new, based on the value that we place on the event. Value is measured by our expected pleasure or reward. It is called the dopamine response. Dopamine is a neurotransmitter in our brain that records experiences and drives us toward a pleasurable response based on a certain stimulus. The value we place on an event will drive us toward or away. We will decide to try it or deny it.

Drug or tobacco addiction violates common sense. The dopamine response overrides common sense. People are not born with the desire to use tobacco or drugs. But hallucinogenic drugs have been used for centuries. Common sense says, "Don't breath in smoke." Uncommon sense says, "Some smoke makes me feel good." Some people value the event—feeling better with smoke.

If we place a high enough value on trying something new, we move on. If we perceive little value, we stay put. What was the perceived value of eating the turtle eggs in the jungle in Honduras? I did not want to embarrass the commander, and I wanted to engage his friendship (see chapter 7, "It's OK to Be Bad").

Move On or Stay Put: Risk versus Benefit

Even though we may assign value to an event, our final decision will be based on the risk-to-benefit ratio. Low risk, high value is an easy decision. Eating a nice tender steak is low risk, high value. High risk, low value might be looked upon as raising the needle on the dumb meter, like trying to bite the hind quarter of a steer standing in the pasture.

What would be the risk and benefit of learning to play golf? Risk is that it requires an investment of time and money. Benefit is that you get to meet people, exercise in pleasant surroundings, enjoy many levels of competition, and you can play until you can't see the ball when you hit it. It is low risk and high value. But what if you don't have time and money to invest? Then the risk is high. If you don't like to meet people, hate competition, and want more strenuous exercise, then golf is low value and little benefit to you.

Racing a motorcycle is high risk, low value to me. Won't even try. But to some individuals, they tried it, liked it, and are good at it. The benefits to them outweigh the risk. The risk-to-benefit ratio plays an important role in our decision to move on or stay put.

Common sense gives predicable results. We already know the benefit of using common sense. We justify deviating from common sense based on a perceived benefit. If we deviate from what common sense tells us, will the reward justify the risk? Do we want a predictable or perceived benefit? It's a decision.

Move On or Stay Put: Morality

Is it the right thing to do? It's that gut feeling. It's the feeling that's in your heart. The foundation of the feeling began as an infant and matured with every family, spiritual, and social experience. We were taught to smile, stand, share, socialize, and be strong. We learned right from wrong. Common sense taught us to choose right.

The people around us, the people whom we seek support influence our decisions. A supportive first circle will drive us toward doing the right thing (see chapter 12, "Circles of Influence"). The influence of the second circle usually challenges our decision and may cause us to decide to do the wrong thing. Keep in mind that the important phrase is "cause us to decide." You can't blame the people around you for your decision. You decide to accept or reject their influence. The final decision is yours. Hopefully, the decision to move on or stay put is based on what is right.

Move On or Stay Put: Priority

The hierarchy of the priorities of life are the following (also in chapter 9, "Comfort Zone")

Priority	Provides
1. Our God	Spiritual comfort and well-being
2. Country	Safety and security
3. Family	Safety and security
4. Plan A	Provides food, clothing, and shelter
5. Personal events	Everything else that we do
6. Plan B	Provides lifestyle

Our decision to move on or stay put must serve our priorities. Our spirituality is the lifeline that sustains us as we progress through the priorities of life. In battle, when fighting for your country, you won't find an atheist in a foxhole.

Playing golf and missing your child's second birthday party is putting one personal event before another person event.

But golfing with the boss when vying for a promotion and missing the birthday party may be putting a personal event before Plan A. Golfing with the boss when vying for a promotion instead of being with your child who is having surgery would be putting Plan A above family.

Priorities Can Change

When we set and understand our priorities, we make better decisions. Some people have to make priority decisions based on the circumstances at the moment. The circumstances at the time and common sense can modify or justify the action. The question is, will the event take me toward my overall goal or mission? Does it fall within and support my priorities?

Years ago, my wife and I would go for drives in the country. We were newlyweds and had time. When we came to an intersection, we would ask, "Left, right or straight?" Our priority was just to be together, see the countryside, and have fun. Had our priority been to get from point A to point B, left, right, or straight ahead would demand a better answer. When our priority changed to getting back home, we took out a map (GPS didn't exist then) and determined where we were and where we wanted to be. We anticipated the intersection and knew which direction to go before we reached the intersection.

There was plenty of reason to have fear in the turtle egg incident. Was I safe? I was a civilian in a war zone. My leverage was that they needed me to treat the wounded soldiers' facial wounds. I was in a room with twice as many guns and grenades as people. Were all the soldiers on the same team? I thought so, until two days later, when an infiltrator killed a commander standing next to my aide. Just eating raw eggs in a less-than-sanitary environment is a risk. Simply, I had to deal with the fear of the unknown.

The mission was to gain access to medical supplies. The priority was to establish rapport with this commander. He controlled the black market that controlled most of the supplies that I needed in order to do surgery. This was a high-priority personal event. Priority one. Complete the mission. Swallow and smile.

Priorities will change as we learn more about the events before us. They add action, motivation, and persistence. Priority paints the final decision with the banner of success.

Move On or Stay put: My Final Decisions

Priorities: College. When my priority changed from attending college to qualifying to get into dental school, my grades changed.

Priorities: Dental School. When the priority was to be the best dentist that I could be and have options to choose any specialty, I graduated in the top 5 of my class.

Risk to benefit: Serving my country. The risk was there, but the benefit of helping my comrades at arms far outweighed the risk.

Value the event: Five more years of training. It was the investment of time and family that would allow me to help people with facial deformities, provide for my family, and develop surgery procedures that became the foundation of surgery today.

Risk to benefit: Starting new businesses. Starting businesses provided income diversification and long-term security for my family.

Value the events: Supporting kids and grandkids. Being there for them. Provide inspirational, educational, and motivational support in their pursuit of successful careers.

Value the event: Giving back. Helping people in business. Choosing to help people understand the principles of business. Coaching them through failures on their way to success.

Risk to benefit: What's next? We will see what tomorrow brings

D.Mata 2014

Chapter 6

Grandfather's Handbook

Andy came home to his apartment. It was late. He was tired. He just slumped back on the couch.

What a day. Finally, he could say he was a graduate of Georgia Tech. He would never say it was easy, but he was proud that he made it. There were times when he almost quit. There were times when he thought he might want to change his major. But he always remembered what GP told him about setting goals. He said to always keep your goal in front of you. Focus on your goal and you will have the best chance of reaching it. Lose focus and it's like throwing a ball up in the air and then trying to catch it with your eyes closed.

He said that the toughest part of a mountain climber's climb is the last ten feet. He is tired and weak. Oxygen is low, and his body is telling him to stop. If he stops, he fails. Failure is not measured in inches; it is measured by achievement. You succeed or fail. If the player fails to catch the ball, he doesn't get credit for an "almost catch." He gets a credit for a miss. The climber either reaches the top or he doesn't. The climber can see the top. He can see the reason for his climb. The climber stays focused and reaches the top. Grandpa was right. And Andy was now a graduate with a degree in aeronautical engineering.

During those four years, he and GP spent many visits just talking about things. They always started out about nothing but ended with some little point that Andy thought about after the visit. Sometimes Andy would have questions for GP. Rarely did he have a chance to ask them. They just talked. But every time he thought about the visit with GP, he found that GP had answered his questions. They talked about nothing, but GP knew it was something.

The Picture Frame

When Andy was in high school, GP taught Andy about the picture frame. He asked Andy to draw a rectangle on a paper. This was a picture frame, and the picture was of Andy's future. He told Andy that whatever he put in the picture frame, he could have. Andy thought GP was cool. All he had to do was draw it in the picture and he could get it.

Andy asked if he could put a motorbike in the picture. GP told him to put it in the picture. He could put anything that he wanted, and he would get it. A motorbike. A pick-up truck. Ball glove. Golf clubs. Girlfriend. Mary C. (he was getting specific). His own room. GP told him to think about five years from now, and if everything went perfect, what would he want his picture to look like?

This was fun. Andy put in his girlfriend. Finished college. Better, bigger pick-up truck. Porsche. Airplane. Beach house. Kids. African safari. Help Grandpa (good choice). Andy was getting excited. GP was really a great guy! He knew that GP was going to see that Andy had all the things in the picture. He didn't want to seem greedy, but if it was OK with GP, he wanted to add a few more things. Anything he wanted was fine with GP. He kept asking GP if he really could have all the things in his picture. Grandpa would smile and tell him to add it to the picture.

When there was no room left in the picture, GP let Andy expand the edges of the picture. This was great. More room meant more things. When Andy finally finished, he was excited and exhausted. This was the neatest thing GP had ever done for Andy. He wondered why GP hadn't offered to get him all these things before. Maybe GP won the lottery or maybe he just had all this money that no one knew that he had.

After a while, Andy asked when GP was going to start delivering all the things on the list. GP asked him to just put a delivery date down next to each one of the items in the picture. This was really fun! He would clear a place in the garage tomorrow so that he would have room for the motorbike. He put the date of graduation from college. He wrote down the Piper Comanche's tail number and the color of his pick-up. He got stuck on the kids. Two boys or two girls or one of each or maybe two of each.

GP looked on and then left the room. Andy was busy. When GP returned, he settled Andy and told him a story about the picture frame. The story goes that GP was speaking to a small group of businessmen and businesswomen. They had concerns about being in business for themselves and the challenges some of them were facing in their businesses. GP had met most of them, but they did not know each other. He had asked them to get together because he felt there was a common theme in their business anxieties.

GP talked about having a good business plan and then following the plan. He explained that some people start a business but can't explain how the business is supposed to work. Others start their business and then don't follow the plan. If you ask them what they thought of a man with a map who still gets lost, they will shake their heads and wonder why he doesn't just follow the map—follow the business plan! This is a common problem in business start-ups.

He talked about sticking to the business plan but being flexible in its execution. So what happens if the man with the map comes to a detour? He has some choices. He can drive through the detour and crash. He can turn around and go back, or he can take the detour and still get to his destination. In business, detours are common. The good businessman takes the detour. His business plan is intact. He simply has modified its execution.

Life in Progress

He looked at the audience, and even though they were attentive and polite, he didn't feel that he was getting through to them. He felt they would leave without answers. Over the years GP had kept a written list of the things he wanted to accomplish.

Each item also had a completion date. GP looked at his list often and made changes mostly to dates but sometimes to add, to erase, or to check off items. His list was a work in progress. You might say it was a "life in progress." Maybe he could share his technique of listing the things you want to accomplish before you set out to accomplish them. He would teach them to know where you want to go before you start your journey.

He had the audience take a break. He said that when they came back, he had something very special to share with them. When they returned, they all sat anxiously to hear what was coming. He said that he was going to talk to them about dreams and goals. Moans and groans. He wasn't surprised, but he knew he was now on the right track.

Most people don't like to talk about their dreams and goals. Even though they may have them, they spend more time telling themselves why they can't have something rather than how they can get it. GP loves to talk to people about how they see themselves in the future. It often takes a few minutes, but eventually they will share their dream. He doesn't give them a chance to tell him why they can't reach their dream. He just tells them that he is confident that they will make it.

"Is it important to you? Tell me what you are doing to get there. How is it going so far? You will make it." He was simply entrenching their dream and challenging them to go for it.

So the audience's response was not unusual. GP pulled out a well-used piece of paper, wrinkled, marked, and erased. He explained that this was his dream list, which he has used for many years. He had their attention. Every item on the list was either completed, deleted, or a work in progress. He let them touch it. It was like a little spark to each person as they looked at the items. Toys. Tools. Trips. Family. Fun. Failures and successes. All the items written on a simple piece of paper. A life in progress.

After a few minutes and listening to their comments, he heard the answer to their business anxiety. They began to talk about how he simply wrote down what he wanted to have before he went out to get it. They wanted to know more.

GP asked them what they thought about a man who went to the airport ticket counter and simply asked for a ticket but wouldn't tell the agent where he wanted to go. If the agent asked you where you wanted to go and you told him, "Anywhere would be fine," other than calling for security, he might just print a ticket. How would you know which gate, which plane, and which seat you were assigned? You would simply look at the ticket. Actually, you would have to look at the ticket to find out where you were going. The ticket agent decided where you would end up when you completed your trip. You paid the price, you completed the journey, but the agent determined the destination.

In life, we have a choice. We are going to pay the price regardless. We all will make the journey. That's life. But we have a choice as to where the journey will take us. We can let life determine our destination, or we can tell life the destination that we wish to reach. When you tell the ticket agent where you want to go, he can only give you a ticket to get there. There is no guarantee that you will get there with that ticket. But with the right ticket, you have the best chance of getting there. The audience was now listening. Tickets? Journeys? Destinations? What was GP talking about?

It got worse. GP asked them to think about the guy who never went to the ticket counter to get a ticket. He would never get on a plane. He would never take a trip. He would always stay in one place. GP explained that in life, we are always on the journey. Life moves us around every day. Life has us getting older every day. Life has us interacting with people every day. And life forces us to make decisions every day.

Life forces us to make decisions for survival. When we go beyond food, clothing, and shelter, life gives us the option to look down, look up, and look ahead. We can look at where we have been, we can look at where we are, and we can look at where we are going. Life offers that we can't change where we have been or where we are. But like the ticket agent, if we want to change where we will be, we simply have to tell the agent where we want to go, and he will give us the right ticket to get there. Life is that agent. Determine where you want to go, and life will get you the ticket that will get you there.

Writing Your Ticket

He asked the audience to take out a piece of paper. He had them list the things that they wanted to have in their lives over the next year. A second list was for things that they wanted over the next five years. With heads down, the audience quietly worked on their list. While they wrote, GP talked about things that he had on his list. He shared that it is important to put anything and everything that they may want to have in their future. Trips. Toys. Family. Friends. Future. Money. Retirement.

GP talked about some of his dreams and how he had to change them, thus the erasure marks on his paper. He shared that most of the erase marks were from changing the completion dates. He had many detours along the way. Sometimes, he simply had to learn more. That meant learning a skill or, in many cases, just learning more about GP himself. Personal growth. Success's playbook and failure's excuse book. Sometimes he had to find help from other people. That meant developing the people skills that would build relationships. He found that he could accomplish his dreams and goals when he helped people accomplish their dreams and goals. He said the detours were not barriers or roadblocks. They were simply direction signs necessary to help us get to our destination.

Grandpa Learns a Life Lesson

The audience had come alive. There was excitement, hope, and confidence in their eyes. GP was confident he was going to be able to help everyone attain the business success that they wanted. He was sure that he would be able to help them go with confidence in every aspect of their lives. Grandpa was becoming a figment of his own imagination. He forgot about a saying that he used many times: "If you think you know, you probably don't. If you think you know everything, you don't."

Sure, it was in the back of his mind somewhere, but it probably didn't apply to him.

He asked if anyone would like to come up and share their list with the rest of the audience. One by one they presented their dreams and goals. It was exciting. With each presentation, the audience applauded. It was like everyone was cheering for each other's success. What a powerful display. Everyone is a player, and everyone is a cheerleader. We don't see that very often in our daily lives. Everyone is a player, but it's hard to find cheerleaders.

GP knew that when the people left the presentation, they would be leaving these cheerleaders. They would be back into the world of the NIOP (negative influence of other people). In order to emphasize the importance of not letting people determine their future and steal their dreams, GP asked them to pass their lists to the front. When he had their lists, he held them up so that they could see them.

He said, "These lists are the tickets to your future. You have written your ticket and you can't let anyone take it away from you."

The audience just looked at him. He was not smiling. They began to realize that they had given away the ticket to their future. Would you give away your lottery tickets before the numbers were announced? Of course not! Why did the audience simply pass their lists to the front? It was because they had not yet appreciated the value of their lists. GP held the lists and then asked them to share with each other how important their personal list was to them. He watched as some said they would simply make another list while others felt it was almost a sacred document.

It is important to understand that this is your own personal ticket. It is for your seat on the plane. No one else can sit there, even if they want to share the ride and destination. Then GP admits he made one of the dumbest mistakes. He wanted to demonstrate just how personal and important these lists are to the individual. He began to tear them up, one at a time. One by one the pieces fell to the floor.

He said the audience became quiet. Then there were a few quiet comments. They became restless in their seats. The pieces began to form a pile of litter around his feet. They floated down in an irregular pile. Their comments became louder.

"Why are you tearing them up? We worked hard on them," they shouted.

Grandpa looked at them. They were serious. They were upset! He had to gain his composure. He realized that he had hurt the very people that he was trying to help. He had dashed their dreams. He did the very thing that he said other people will do to them. He felt terrible. He began to apologize.

The audience became restless. They wanted their dreams back. They wanted their share of the pieces of paper on the floor. GP slowly bent down, picked as many as he could, held them in front of him, and said, "I am truly and sincerely sorry. I didn't mean to hurt any of you."

There was quiet. Then one man stood up and said the he will make a new list. They looked at him, and then another and another echoed his sentiment. They realized that they determine their future. They learned that even if someone tries to steal their dreams, they can dream again. Anger and resentment toward GP started to turn to respect and appreciation. GP wanted to make the point that they ultimately learned. To this day, he regrets the way he hurt the people he was trying to help.

Andy's List

Andy's list was on the table as GP finished his story. He thought that GP pulled a mean trick on those people. What was GP going to do to him? GP explained that over the years, every one of the people in the audience not only learned how to make and maintain their list, but they also learned to protect it. No different than the traveler who guards his map or the chef who protects his recipe.

If you do lose it or someone takes it, you made it and you can make it again. Andy was curious as to who might take his list. GP smiled. He knew Andy was getting the picture. Most people lose their list to the little guy next to the guy who created it. Both are between your ears. There will be times when you think you are going the wrong way because it is a little difficult. There may be NIOP's along the way who don't understand your mission. They will want to keep you where *they* are comfortable with you.

If you see your dog barking and running all around the yard, don't shoot him. He may be on the scent of the rabbit that went through the yard an hour ago. He has vision and a mission. You are blind and don't understand the mission. People will be the same way. They don't know what or why you are doing what you do. They don't know where you are going, and they don't understand what you have to do to get there. In the end, you get what you want, and so what if they don't understand it? They're probably not willing to "write their own ticket."

A Special Gift

Andy rested on the couch, thinking about the busy day. The whole family was in town for the graduation. Tomorrow morning they would have breakfast, and then everyone would be heading home. He wished his buddy, Grandpa, could have seen him go across the stage. It would have made it a perfect day.

GP is in his seventies, so he has a little issue getting around. Andy was glad he called that morning just to say hi and wish him well. GP sounded so happy for Andy. He was Andy's hero.

It was after eleven already when there was a knock at the door. What now? Andy opened the door, and his neighbor was standing there.

"I'm really sorry to bother you, Andy," he said. "I saw the light on, and I knew this was important, so I took a chance that you were still up."

He said, "An elderly man stopped by this afternoon and left this package for you. He had a lady with him, but they said they couldn't wait for you. They wanted me to make sure that I gave you this package."

Andy thanked the neighbor. Who was the old man with the lady? he wondered. The package was wrapped in brown paper and Scotch tape. The label said, "For Andy." Andy removed the wrapping and opened the box. It was a three-inch binder filled with papers. On the front was written in a wide blue marker, "Grandpa's Notes."

Near the bottom it said, "A Grandfather's Handbook."

Andy just stared at the cover. He slowly opened the cover, and a note fell to the floor. In a shaky script the note said,

> *Andy,*
>
> *I know this day is so important to you, and I wish I could have been there as your cheerleader. I'm proud of you.*
>
> *These are my notes with both good and bad experiences, most of which you are already familiar.*
>
> *If our talks helped you, I'm humbled. If our talks help you help others, I'm blessed.*
>
> *You are a very special guy. Keep your picture frame in front of you. Your success will be your decision. You will make things happen.*
>
> *GP loves you.*

Andy couldn't wait to read Grandpa's notes.

Chapter 7

It's OK to Be Bad

Like the turtle and the hare, it's not how long it takes to get to 10,000 hours; it's that when you reach 10,000 hours, you now have mastered the skill.

Andy opened the book to look at GP's notes. They were mostly typed with handwritten notations in the margins. It seemed like he was constantly adding his thoughts. Some entries had a group or person's name and date in the margins indicating when he discussed the topic. GP always wanted to use one topic as the foundation for the next. That's probably why he kept track of his talks to different groups and organizations.

Andy thumbed through the pages until "It's OK to Be Bad"

caught his eye. He remembered when GP would tell him that it's OK to be bad at something so long as you are willing to try again. You can't become good at something until you are bad at it. The first time you try something new will be the worst you will be. It gets better with practice as long as you practice the right things.

Andy remembered the story of GP learning to pound nails. When he was a little boy, like most little boys, he liked to hammer things. His dad let him hammer until he was good enough at hammering that he was starting to break things. GP wanted to pound nails like his dad and the other men. They would drive nails into the boards while GP just made noise pounding on the boards.

One day, GP's dad gave him some nails. GP held the nail and gave it a good whack. The nail bent, so GP grabbed another, then another, and another until all his nails were bent. GP was sure it wasn't his hammering. It must be the hammer, or the nails, or the wood, or most likely the wind. When he asked for more nails, his dad told him to straighten out the bent nails and try again. Why couldn't he just get some more straight nails? It was because he was good at hammering and bending nails. He was bad at driving nails into the boards.

At that point, GP would have to develop the skill of driving nails. If not, he would resign himself to being a bad nail driver. His dad made him straighten the bent nails and use them again. Straightening a bent nail requires some skill. Accuracy is motivated by the fear of hitting your finger. Hit your finger with a hammer enough times and you become very accurate and precise with the hammer! That accuracy also helped master the skill of driving a nail into an oak board without bending it.

GP said he learned that if he wanted to drive with the big boys, he would have to practice. He would have to learn what they know and do. Even if it meant a bandage on every finger. He had to be bad at driving a nail into the board before he could ever be good at it. If he saw all the carpenters with bandaged or bloody fingers, he might have never tried to use a hammer. If his father saw him bend the nail, his dad might have encouraged him to use a screwdriver.

GP told us that people have all kinds of reasons or excuses to try or not to try something. Sometimes they are simply afraid. Their fear may be based on knowledge, but often it is based on perceptions from lack of knowledge. He said some people are afraid to go to the dentist because they think they will experience pain. When asked if they have ever felt pain in a dental office, they report that they have never been to a dental office. So how can they be afraid? It is a perception of pain based on information from people who don't know. Millions and millions of people seek dental treatment every day. He said that most do not have any pain at all.

Some people do not see the value of trying something. At a sushi bar, eating raw fish is still an option. If you want to impress your girlfriend, try the fish. If you are with Mom and Dad, try the baked salmon. They don't need to be impressed. There may be little value in eating raw fish unless you are stranded on a lifeboat for a few weeks. A fish of any kind might be worth a try.

We always have to assess the risk-to-benefit ratio of trying something. When GP's dad wanted him to climb the ladder to handpick the pears, a perfect pear versus a broken leg was an important consideration. GP said he liked pears, so he climbed the ladder. His dad told him that if the ladder started to fall, GP was to ride it down until it was about three feet from the ground and then jump off. He told GP that no one ever got hurt jumping just three feet. I never understood the logic, and GP never explained. He really did like those pears.

GP told us that some people try things and later find themselves in trouble. It might be something that is illegal. It might be something that is harmful to them or the people around them. Think of the people who are addicted to drugs, tobacco, sex, or alcohol. They had to try it once. The question that they had to answer was, is this right or wrong? GP said over and over that he wanted us to know the difference between right and wrong and always choose right.

GP told us that there is usually a good time and bad time to try things. Singing your favorite country song is better done in the shower rather than during the preacher's sermon. A solo is best during a chorus concert rather than when GP is trying to impart his tremendous wisdom. In our picture frame exercise, we set times for things to happen. That includes trying new things, learning new skills, and getting better at others.

There are times when we get put into a position where we must try something new. GP told us of the time when he was in Vietnam and wasn't sure he would be able to run if he had to. He had had surgery on both knees, and running was very limited. He was a surgeon, and his work was supposed to be in a hospital. There wouldn't be any need to run in the hospital. After three days in country, he was sent on temporary duty to a small dispensary in the Mekong Delta.

He was told that he should know where the nearest bunker was at all times. When the siren goes off, take cover in the bunker. That meant running. He wasn't sure he could run, and how fast wasn't even considered. It was about 10:00 p.m. on his second day in the delta. A series of rapid explosions were followed by the wail of the siren. The base was under attack. GP said he was out the door in a flash. Was he trying to run? Trying wasn't an option. He was full speed.

After the attack, things settled down. He heard one of the corpsman commenting on how fast that new captain ran for the bucker. One said that he must have played football or ran track. GP didn't try to run. Try was not an option. Fear, value, risk, and morality were all motivating. As to priority, it was the highest priority on GP's mind at the time.

The Turtle Incident

GP has some interesting stories about being forced to try something new. This was more of being forced into a situation rather than doing something bad in hopes of getting better. GP was working with the International Medical Corps treating facial wound injuries for the contra freedom fighters in Honduras.

Grandpa's Notes

There are times when we are forced to try new things. The first time I had turtle eggs, it was not something I picked on the menu. I was in a camp in the jungles of Honduras working on wounded soldiers. A contra commander had asked me to come to his headquarters to discuss my work and the need for the supplies that I had requested.

The room with a dirt floor and holes in the wall for light was about 15 × 15 feet with a small table and four chairs in the center. At least ten armed soldiers stood around the perimeter of the room. There were no smiles. Just stares. The aide pointed to where I was to sit. I took my chair and waited for the commander.

When he entered the room, the soldiers came to attention. I stood to shake his hand.

Although I was a little on edge, I managed to smile. He was quite disarming and actually made me feel comfortable. After a few minutes, the aide brought out two glasses. "I hope you like turtle eggs," he said.

What do you say to your host when he has ten men with guns looking over your shoulder? I could have considered sterility and passed. I could have considered the fact that turtles may become extinct and take a moral position that we must protect the species. I could have considered the taste, consistency, and digestive course that these raw eggs would present. I could have explained that he doesn't understand that I may not like turtle eggs. I could have thought about the relationship that may develop if I accept his hospitality. I could have just said to myself, "If it won't hurt him, it won't hurt me. I'll be fine."

We each picked up our glass for the toast. I peeked over the top of my little glass. Two egg yolks floated at the bottom of the tequila. A large red dab of hot sauce floated on top of the tequila. Our eyes fixed on each other. (It's like a guy thing at the highest level. Who will blink first?) Glasses to our lips, gone were the eggs, the tequila, and the hot sauce. Our glasses clicked on the table. He smiled, and I knew we were in business.

What were the chances that I would get better at eating raw turtle eggs? Slim to none. The thing that saved the day was that I was not afraid to try. I considered the options and alternatives, made a decision, and had turtle eggs for the first and last time in my life, so far.

When I look back at that experience, before I picked up the glass with the turtle eggs, I had to calm my fears, accept the value of the event, understand the risks involved, make sure that this was the right thing to do, and finally decide if this was the time to act. I guess it was. We helped a lot of young men over the course of the war.

When It's OK to Be Bad at Something

It's OK to be bad at something so long as you are willing to try again. If you don't try again, you will always be bad at it. I've heard people say, "He's good at everything he does"—not talking about me, for sure. I wonder if they really believe it, or is it just an excuse for them not to try to be better themselves?

When I was fifteen, I asked my dad, a natural athlete, to teach me to golf. When he swung the club, it was smooth. When I would swing the club, it was erratic, and I missed the ball. I exclaimed that the club did not feel comfortable. I felt that I was really bad at golf.

Dad agreed that I had a bad swing. He agreed that the club felt uncomfortable. He even expressed reservations that I would be able to hit the ball. But he never said I would be a bad golfer. He said, "You have to be bad at something before you can ever be good at something." He explained that people who are bad at something and never try again will always be bad at it.

When Dad was a youngster, there weren't any TVs. Kids in the neighborhood played ball every day during the summer and evenings and weekends during the school year—softball, baseball, football, kickball, tennis, and even golf. As he got older, he caddied at the county club and learned the game.

How many pitches did he throw until he was good enough to be recruited by the Pittsburgh Pirates in 1940? How many strikes did he have before he was consistently hitting fastballs? I remember when Dad played in as many as three softball leagues during the same season.

I don't think Dad was a natural athlete. I believe he just studied and practiced the game more than anyone around him. So do we have natural athletes, or do we have individuals who have become good athletes by developing and practicing their skills?

10,000 Hours

Geoff Colvin's book *Talent Is Overrated* gives hope to anyone who wants to get better at any task. Research showed that it takes about 10,000 hours to master a skill or what we may call a talent. They concluded that anyone who commits to developing a skill or talent could succeed.

Conversely, someone who shows a propensity for a certain skill and at five years old can hit a baseball but who becomes satisfied that he is a natural and does not practice will be passed by the eight-year-old who just learned to hit the ball a year ago.

Example: Two individuals who start on their 10,000-hour journey may work at different paces. At any given point in time, one may appear more talented because he has more hours of practice. If 10,000 hours of practice takes five years to accomplish, that person will appear to have more talent. Like the story of the turtle and the hare, it's not how long it takes to get to 10,000 hours; it's that when you reach 10,000 hours, you now have mastered the skill.

The key to the successful development of a skill or talent is to never quit practicing/growing. If there is any credence to a natural talent, I will still opt for the individual who is willing to develop and grow over the "natural talent" who doesn't need to practice anymore.

I've seen very talented young people give up on their gift, change focus, and start to develop a new skill or talent. Even though they are good at their first talent, they will now start out bad as they develop their new skill. It is important to recognize that just because you are good at one thing, it does not mean that you will automatically be good at something else. Developing the new skill/talent will require the same amount of work/practice/study as the first skill/talent.

We have to become bad at something before we can become good at something. The difference between bad and good is a function of *vision, focus, commitment*, and *time*. We already recognize that a baby's first step does not have to be perfect. Even when the baby falls down, we encourage him to get up and get his steps in order. He must be a bad walker before he becomes a good walker.

Can you imagine a parent saying, "Well, it looks like we have another bad walker. At least we'll save money on shoes. He can just crawl around." Not acceptable. We commit to helping the child learn to walk. We practice. He develops the walking skill. If we continue, the child may become a runner or dancer, a talent way beyond learning to walk.

So when is it OK to be bad? When we are willing to try again. We get better through practice and repetition. But we have to start somewhere. The second time will be better than the first time. We have to be bad at something before we can be good at it.

The four functions to get from bad to good:

1. Vision
2. Focus
3. Commitment
4. Time

Vision: Know where you want to go and what you want to achieve. The more one can define the goal, the greater the possibility of reaching the goal. A student in his freshman year who sees himself in his career position after graduation has the best chance to accomplish that goal. A student without vision attends rather than participates in his education. His vision is graduation. A student with a vision sees graduation as the beginning of his professional career. Visualize what you want to accomplish. Picture yourself crossing the finish line.

Focus: Focus, by definition, clears our vision. It allows attention to detail. Focus blocks out anything that can blur your vision. Focus alleviates distractions. But focus is not automatic. It requires a decision. Once you have vision, you know where you want to go, focus will lay out and keep you on the right path.

Commitment: Commitment is the energy that drives success. Developing sufficient energy can be one of the major hurdles to achieving success, to becoming good at something. Are you willing to commit all the resources necessary to become successful? Success requires a decision that is powered by a priority. Making the commitment simply means that achieving success is now the highest priority. Marriage is not just a piece of paper or a few words in front of a group of friends. Marriage requires a commitment to work in order to sustain a lasting relationship. Marriage without commitment is nothing more than a couple of people getting along so long as they are comfortable. A team that wins depends on a commitment to win from every team member. An individual who wins depends on a personal commitment to win. Commitment energizes!

A lady asked me how long I had gone to school to become a surgeon. I said, "Thirteen years after high school."

"My goodness, I would never spend that long in school," she replied.

"Then you will never be a surgeon. It's as simple as that."

Set the priority.

Time: Time is a commodity available to invest. We all have the same twenty-four hours each day to invest in ourselves. Like eating an elephant, one bite at a time, it may take 10,000 bites. It can be a bite a month, a bite a day, or a bite an hour. It still takes 10,000 bites to eat the elephant. The good news is that if you need 10,000 hours to go from bad to good, to reach your goal, you control the investment.

Based on how you invest your time, you determine when you will reach your goal. If you only need 1,000 hours to accomplish your goal, committing one hour a month would take 83 years (start young). One hour a week = 20 years (still hope). Or one hour a day = 2 years 7 months (start now). Your individual goal may not take 1,000 hours, but it will still require an investment of your time. If it is 100, 1,000, or 10,000 hours, success still requires a 100 percent investment. Anything less can only make you "not bad and almost good."

These four elements will move us from bad to good. Quitting interrupts the 10,000-hour journey to success. People who we recognize as leaders, successful businessmen, athletes or entertainers will describe long hours of practice, study, and mentoring in order to reach their success. They will also report many opportunities to quit. They will report failures that became learning experiences as they went from bad to good. It's OK to be bad on your way to being good. Don't quit. Just try again!

Andy put the book down for a moment. He remembered complaining to Grandpa about his golf grip. Grandpa sure had a way with words. He told him that if it was comfortable when a person first picked up a golf club, then everyone would be walking around with a golf club in his or her hand.

After reading Grandpa's notes, it made a little more sense why he always asked people what they were up to. He liked to hear that they were doing something that would help them grow. Was it a book? A new class? A new hobby? Whatever it was, he congratulated them and encouraged them to continue.

Grandpa felt that trying something new energizes a person. He said that learning new things creates new pathways in the brain. It's like the first explorers that went out west. They created a pathway that, years later, turned into a parkway. New pathways in the brain become parkways for new information to be stored and retrieved. Grandpa just wanted people to continue to grow. The alternative was scary.

Andy took a quick break. This stuff was good. It was making sense.

Chapter 8

Trees

A leader steps out, succeeds, and then uplifts the people around him.

Andy couldn't wait to pick up the book. He remembered one time he and Grandpa were headed to pick blueberries in the country. He saw a couple of deer out in the pasture. Under a big tree were a bunch of cows lying in the shade. Both the deer and the cow were enjoying the day. One cow was scratching against the trunk of the tree.

Andy mentioned that if they kept pushing on the tree, the cows could knock the tree over. Grandpa pointed out that if it were not for the cows pushing on the tree, the tree wouldn't be there. He said that when the cows pushed on the trunk of the tree, the roots became stronger. It didn't make sense. Then grandpa explained with his *tree* story.

Grandpa liked to point out the simple things that we could learn by observing nature. How did people learn before we had the benefits of research, books, and history? They learned by looking around. They learned to look at the sky to understand seasons. They learned to plant, harvest, store food, and seek shelter by observing the sky and the appearance and movement of the clouds.

They knew whether to hunt or hide by looking at the worn paths in the forest. Small footprints meant food for a day. Big footprints meant get a bigger bow and arrow or hide. Big footprints also meant food for the winter. Nature told them that they could harvest some plants in a few months while others took years. Fathers taught their sons. Mothers taught their daughters. Elders taught the next generation.

Producers and Nonproducers

He said that as communities started to develop, people became dependent on one another. Some became the fisherman and farmers that produced the food. Some became builders. Some made clothes. They were the producers. The people decided that they needed someone to organize and manage the village activities while they worked. They were the non-producers. It was the beginning of a government. Grandpa loved to talk about the government. He said, "Remember that the government doesn't produce anything. It can only redistribute what it takes from someone else. And it always keeps a little for itself."

In the village, the nonproducers made sure that the fishermen shared their catch with the rest of the people. The farmers had to share their crops with the community. The builders built the houses and roads, and the nonproducers saw that they had food. One day the fisherman didn't catch many fish. The nonproducers got first pick since they had to give fish to the rest of the village. The fishermen found that they didn't have enough fish for their own families.

Some went back out to the sea to find more fish for their family. When they returned, the nonproducer was there waiting. Even though the fishermen were just going out to get some fish for their own family, the nonproducer took the fish back to the village. After all, the nonproducers had to eat too.

Grandpa said that the lesson to learn is, first, that the government doesn't produce anything and they will always get their cut first. And second, and most important, you must take care of you and your family first.

The fishermen and the farmers learned to keep some fish and grain in a separate barrel so that they could feed their families. The butchers and bakers kept some meat and bread behind the counter for their families. When the bricklayers and the blacksmiths couldn't get food for their families from the government, they traded their services with the farmers and fishermen for food.

The village people redefined the role of their government (nonproducers). They wanted the government to provide for the safety and defense of the village. They were willing to give some of their food and services for the common and specific needs of all the people. They were specific that the people (producers) would determine the needs and the government (nonproducers) would administer to the need.

When danger threatened the village, everyone became part of the defense. The elders in the village taught the people that there were some villages in which the people couldn't produce enough to meet the need of their government. Their leaders told the people that there were other villages that had food. Since the government was in the business of taking, it would just take the food from the other villages.

Since the people were happy to have the government provide all their food, they agreed with the leader. They thought that it was only fair to take the food from the producers (working people) and provide for the nonproducers. Grandpa said that some people believe that "what's mine is mine and what's yours is mine too."

He asked, "Did you ever see two little kids eating cookies? They both have the same cookies, but one always wants a bite of the other one's cookie. It makes you wonder if governments are like kids, only with guns and bullets."

Provide for the Common Defense

When the village was in danger, it affected everyone. That meant that everyone would have to step up to defend the village. The leaders would organize, but the people had to fight. So now we see that there are two basic needs to sustain a village: food and shelter or sustenance and safety.

Danger came from both outside and within the village. When they had to defend against the nonproducing villages, they formed an army. Everyone participated. When it was necessary to defend the people against individual nonproducers within the village, they developed a justice system.

The system protected the producers from the nonproducers. People recognized that they had rights and responsibilities. With every right that they had, someone else had the responsibility to provide it. It became apparent that only the people themselves could provide and protect their rights.

Over time, as a village becomes larger, it is important that there is balance between the producers and the nonproducers. Nonproducers ultimately decrease the number of producers. They discourage or dis-incentivize the producers. If left alone, there will always be producers because they understand the motivation of sustenance and safety. They take responsibility for themselves and then for others. Nonproducers take responsibility for themselves *at the expense of others.*

The Country Boy Meets the City Girl

Grandpa loved to tell the story about his first city girlfriend. He had come to the city to go to college. He was amazed that nothing was growing. Everything was concrete and bricks. He had a flowerpot on his desk by the window. He tried to grow some lettuce, but all he got was "try." He missed the farm.

He was happy to see that his next-door neighbor had an interest in agriculture. He recognized the winemaking facility in the basement of the house. Boxes of grapes were discretely lowered down the basement coal chute. He noticed that people stopped by several times a day, probably just to visit, but always left with a heavy box or brown bag that they carefully put in the trunk of their car.

The city girl liked beautiful new shoes. The country boy had work shoes and church shoes. School shoes varied based on the time between morning chores and catching the school bus. The city girl had perfectly painted nails. The country boy just wanted to have most of the grease off his fingers. The nicks and cuts were in all stages of healing. The city girl liked pretty dresses. The country boy liked pretty girls in pretty dresses!

When Grandpa met Patty, it was a big change. She was pretty, loud, and full of energy. It was somewhat overwhelming, but he thought that that's the way they grew them in the city. She seemed to talk at fifty miles an hour with gusts up to eighty. It was an experience between amazement, curiosity, and entertainment. The best part was that she also had a car. GP still hadn't figured out how the streetcars knew where he wanted to go. He had tried them twice and ended up in a strange part of town.

Grandpa's experience with a girlfriend was pure country. He saw how his mom and dad respected each other. His grandparents were the nobility. The family supported one another, but political debates or cheering sporting events were lively. Some ended in, "I'm never coming back." But the next weekend, they were sitting together again debating another subject. He learned to respect people and his lady friend. To that extent, he named one of his prize heifers after his first country girlfriend.

A heifer named Joy. Grandpa was sure Joy Lee felt honored, or he thought she should have been. He never saw much of Joy after the announcement. I'm talking about the girlfriend, not the heifer. The heifer grew up to be a prize cow and won prizes at the county farm shows. Joy Lee, the girlfriend, probably cried every time she saw her namesake's picture with a blue ribbon in the newspaper!

Patty was excited to meet Grandpa's family. They drove about fifty miles to the family farm. Patty kept talking about how there was nothing around. "Where do you shop for clothes? Where do you go to the movies? Where can you buy shoes? I don't know how you can survive out here." She went on and on. She couldn't understand why we didn't have any corner stores. Then she realized that we didn't have any corners, just dirt and asphalt roads between the farms.

When GP's brothers and sisters met Patty, there were chuckles. They never saw anyone like this. She explained how nice it is in the city. When you need something, you can go to the store. The kids knew that trips to the store were planned and that most of the things that Patty bought in the store, Mom, Dad, and the kids made themselves.

The Walk that Became Legend

Grandpa took Patty for a walk to show her all the animals. She had a problem with the smell coming from the chicken coop. So GP couldn't show her where eggs came from. When they got to the barn, the straw on the barn floor was going to scratch her shoes, so she didn't get to see the milking parlor where milk came from. He took her up the barn ramp to the big haymows to smell the fresh alfalfa. She said it smelled like moldy grass. Why would we feed mold to the cows? When he showed her the young wheat field, she thought it would be nicer if we planted grass and kept it mowed.

Grandpa was not making any points with the whirlwind city girl. Finally, he decided to take her down to the family picnic area. It would be a nice place to sit and visit, away from the smells, the scratchy straw, and the rest of the family. The sun was just starting to set, and a light dew was beginning to settle on the grass.

Dad had strung a single-wire electric fence around the area so that the cows could keep the area mowed. When GP and Patty got to the fence, the electric was off, so GP held the fence down for Patty. He told Patty to follow him, but she saw a row of stones that she could walk on. She didn't want to get her shoes wet from the dew on the grass. Before GP could say anything, Patty started stepping on the stones. She knew better.

When all the screaming stopped, GP went over to hold on to Patty. The stones were actually "cow pies," something Patty had never seen. She avoided the dew but was ankle deep in doo-doo. The screaming brought the whole family out to the picnic area. Surprise changed to smiles. Then changed to laughter. GP and his dad lifted Patty out of her shoes and carried her to the water hose on the side of the house.

She was still screaming. "Get this shit off my feet," she yelled over and over. GP thought, "Such pretty toes on such dirty feet!"

Patty never came back to the farm, but her memory will always be there. Most family members loved to hear GP tell the story about his first city girlfriend. Patty never picked up her shoes. They stayed in the cow pies for weeks. GP and the kids would tell people that a big cow ate one of GP's girlfriends and that the shoes were the only things that came out.

GP told the city girl story to contrast city and county living. He said that people were a product of their environment. He compared personalities, values, agendas, and even how they spent their time. Patty and GP were each a product of their environment. Neither was bad. They were just different.

He said that where you will eventually end up in life will be the result of what you have learned in the past and what you did with what you learned. He said that if you want to know what the river will look like, go upstream and see where it is coming from. Each trickle of water adds to the river.

If each trickle comes from the melting snow in the mountain, the river will run pure. If it passes by the village of pollution, it will be as dirty as the village. It is easier to prevent pollution than to remove pollution. The pollution can only be removed downstream. Every experience is like the trickle in the river.

You can predict one's future based on his past. If one's experience pollutes one's future, it must be cleaned. Family, teachers, mentors, education, and good experiences are the filters of pollution. The more filters, the cleaner the river. The more positive experiences and support, the more predictable and positive the future.

Years ago, Grandpa told Andy to just look around. He said, "Look at the trees. Trees tell the whole story."

Andy opened the notebook to see if there really was a story about trees. Sure enough, Grandpa had notes on trees.

Grandpa's Notes

On Trees

Sometimes we can learn a lot by just looking at the things around us. Sometimes we think that we know everything we need to know and why bother with just a little bit more information. But sometimes a little bit more information can make a big difference.

The difference between 211 degrees and 212 degrees is the difference between hot water and steam. Hot water can cook potatoes, but steam can move a train, power a ship, and produce electricity for a whole city. Just a little difference, one degree, makes a big difference.

Looking Around

A lot of what we need to know is available to us by just looking around. My grandpa told me it was harder to knock down one tree standing alone than twenty tall trees standing together. That seemed kind of dumb, but he wasn't talking about trees; he was talking about me growing up to become successful.

He said a tree that stands alone is able to get sun from all sides. This means it can grow all the time. It puts out broader branches in all directions to take advantage of the sun. The roots grow deep and spread out to capture the moisture from the drip line of the leaves.

Trees

Trees that grow in the forest compete for the light and moisture. Their trunks are tall and thin as they reach up for the sun's rays. Their roots compete with the other trees for moisture. The roots do not and cannot spread because of the dense roots from the nearby trees.

Andy thought for a moment. The tree story is talking about the people in city versus the people in the country. The city people are like the trees in the forest. They depend on each other for support. They compete for food in the stores, for seats in the restaurants, parking places, and places in line. They compete for what is available to them. They depend on service for support. The people who are around them limit their vision and experiences. They can only see as far as the person next to them. And like GP's city girlfriend, they can't see how people can survive without the conveniences of the city.

The country people are like the lone tree in the pasture. They can see the whole countryside. They can see and prepare for the upcoming storm. Adversity makes them strong. Nourishment is only limited by how far they can extend their branches and expand their roots. The lone tree does not have to compete for the nourishment in the soil or the sun's rays.

So why would people stay in the city if they are so dependent on their surroundings for survival? It's called the comfort zone. So long as they can afford the conveniences and comforts, they stay. When they can't afford it, they can complain or move.

Complaining only works if there is someone to listen. And that someone might not be able to do anything but listen.

When all the trees in the forest were cut down and the last tree standing didn't have any support, he became the sawdust of the future. People can complain about their situation, but unless they take responsibility for their comforts and conveniences, their comforts and conveniences will be nothing but a comfortable memory.

"Trees can't change their environment, but people can." Andy read on.

Grandpa's Notes

Like the trees, our strength will come from either our foundation or our associations. Our growth will be a function of how much knowledge we can attain and process. A strong foundation will maintain our presence and permits us to seek and process the information around us.

Strength and Growth

The solitary tree gets its strength from broad roots (foundation) and its growth from continued nourishment from the soil and sun (knowledge/learning). Because the tree stands alone, it must deal with all the challenges of nature. The winds try to tip it over, so it spreads its roots. The sun and rain cause more branches and leaves to sprout, so the trunk thickens to hold the weight. When it's about to crack, it bends and then gets stronger. It supports the nesting and resting birds and provides shade and shelter for the cows and deer. It also provides seeds, nuts, and fruit for you and me. One tree, standing alone, does it all, a leader among trees.

The trees in the forest get their strength from each other (association). Because they stand together, the force of the wind is distributed among them. Did you ever notice that when a strong wind attacks the forest, the trees along the edges would fall? It is because they have a small root distribution. Their roots are limited due to competition with the roots of the rest of the trees.

If you cut down all the trees in the forest but one, it will fall at the first wind. People who depend on their support group for survival are like those trees in the forest. As soon as they lose that support (association), they struggle and fail. Leaders are like the solitary tree in the pasture. They can help the other trees grow strong and survive, but the seed must be planted away from the forest. The environment must support a strong foundation.

Growth

The growth of trees in the forest depends on how they can share the nutrients from the soil and sun (rationed knowledge). The amount of sun and rain at any one time must be divided among all the trees. They grow tall to compete for the sun. They are always trying to get higher than the tree beside them. Interesting. It is not too different than when groups of people want to let others get ahead in life, but just not ahead of them.

Family and friends may want you to succeed but only to the level at which they will be comfortable with your success. I'm not sure that it is bad. It is just how people are. A leader steps out, succeeds, and then uplifts the people around him. That's the mark of a real leader. People are better off because of him.

Andy thought about the city people. They are always in a rush. They are always in competition for something. He remembered talking to a friend about his ride to school the other day. Traffic was a little slow, and people were constantly changing lanes to get ahead. Ultimately, they all seemed to get there in due time. No one really got ahead. But it seemed like they just had to compete for position on the highway.

GP used to talk about riding on the country roads. People always waved as they went by. Today, waving at a stranger might generate the return of half of a peace sign. He said that when you were on a dirt road, you slowed down as you approached an oncoming car so that there wouldn't be a lot of dust. Today if you slow down, someone will be beeping at you.

Grandpa's Notes

Fruit for Generations

Another example of nature's message to us can be found in an apple orchard. If the farmer wants a good crop of apples year after year, he plants the trees so that they will not have to compete with the other trees for sun, moisture, and the nutrients in the soil. Too close and the trees can't produce enough fruit. Too far apart and the farmer cannot produce enough fruit to be profitable, to sustain his business.

On the other hand, the farmer who produces trees for lumber plants them close enough to grow but not to branch out. The trees grow tall and are harvested before they produce abundant seeds. Trees in the orchard produce fruit for today and seeds for the next generation. Trees in the forest produce lumber for today. The harvest precludes any seeds for the next generation.

Planting the Seeds

That's not too different from families who instill in their children good family values and teach them to pursue knowledge, to never quit learning. The seeds are planted for the next generation. It's interesting that we see first-generation families in this country that are self-reliant, responsible, and generational in their thinking. They often come from a survival environment with limited or no formal education. Then we find fifth-generation families whose children can't read after receiving a free education. Their survival depends on others, and they feel entitled to convenience, comfort, and happiness.

The first-generation people are like the tree standing alone. They are strong, resourceful, and responsible. The fifth-generation people are like the trees in the forest. They are weak, dependent, and replete with excuses. If we simply want people for this generation only, like the farmer who plants trees for timber for cupboards, then we plant where the seeds compete. If we want people for today AND future generations, like the farmer who plants trees for optimum fruit, then the seeds must be planted in the best environment for growth. We plant the seeds today in order to sustain future generations.

Harvesting the Trees

When we need lumber, we want straight boards. That old tree in the pasture with the thick stumpy trunk and twisted branches is only good for firewood. The short trunk will have huge knots from each of its branches. We leave it alone. Did you ever notice that the old trees in the pasture always have a smile when the sun shines on them? In their final days, they will only be used to keep people warm.

In the woods, however, the trees were tall, few branches and perfect for making long boards. These trees got their support from the others, so they were easy picking. Just one at a time. Trunks were narrow, long, and had few branches. The lumber would be straight and had few knots. The trees never had a chance to get old. As soon as they grew tall, they became a cupboard, chair, or deck.

What's Up, Grandpa?

"What the heck was Grandpa trying to tell me?" thought

Andy. Andy sat there. Where is he going with these trees, seeds, cupboards, and knots? Andy was getting tired, but he couldn't stop.

Grandpa's Notes

If you are going to stand alone, if you want to be successful, if you want to be a leader, then like the tree that stands alone, you must have a strong foundation and never quit growing. That strong foundation will come from the family, from the teachers and mentors that we let become a part of our lives. The growth will come from what we do today and tomorrow to build on that foundation.

Like the tree in the pasture, even with a strong, broad root formation (foundation) that could resist the strongest winds, it will wither and die without light and moisture (knowledge/learning) to feed the leaves and roots. Conversely, without the roots to hold the tree and support the leaves, the sun and rain (knowledge) will be wasted.

If we are going to be leaders, we must start with a broad, strong foundation. When you talk to real leaders, they are humble and always willing to learn. The strong foundation gives them the strength to continue to seek knowledge. They recognize, like the tree that stands alone, that there will always be more sunshine and rain (knowledge) to process. They learn every day.

If we choose to be like the trees in the forest and listen to the people around us, we will grow at their pace. We will never have our head above the crowd. We will never be the tallest tree. And when harvest time comes, we will be like the rest of them, part of someone's cupboard, chair, or deck.

It Takes a Decision

We make decisions every day. The easier decisions give us comfort as we stand among the tall trees around us. Our comfort zone is in the association with others. We live in commonality and resist standing alone. We share the sunshine, compete for the rain, and breathe common air. We grow in concert with our surroundings, carefully not to outgrow those around us. The tough decision is stepping out of the trees and seeing the sun, feeling the rain, and breathing fresh air. Some decisions give us strength, like the tree in the pasture. It is tough to step out.

If the decision is to stand alone, to be a leader, to be the strong tree looking down at all the trees in the forest, our roots must be broad, our trunk must be strong, and our branches must reach out for the sun and rain. We must develop that strong foundation, strong will and commitment, and seek any and all knowledge that will help us grow.

Leadership begins with a decision. "Will I commit to becoming a leader, or will I go with the crowd?" Leadership is lonely. Leadership is humbling. Leadership is tough. But leadership has the reward of helping others to achieve great things. A leader reaches out his hand when people struggle or fail. His puffed-up moment, when he sticks his chest out, is when people succeed.

Andy remembered GP saying, "The tree standing alone in the pasture is stronger than any tree in the forest. *Make a decision to help others succeed and you will have made the first decision toward becoming a leader.*"

Andy closed the notes on trees.

D.Mata 2016

Chapter 9

The Comfort Zone

Before books, our lessons came from nature. There are still lessons out there.

Andy moved on to the next chapter in Grandpa's notebook. These pages looked well worked over. There were corrections, side notes, and inserts. Interesting. Grandpa started out with big letters.

Grandpa's Notes

We can change ... the comfort zone.

We must get comfortable being uncomfortable in order to become comfortable. It's a pattern of success.

Fences, Barriers, Obstacles, Walls

Many people, when asked, will say that they are comfortable. It could be the seat they are sitting on or an assessment of their finances. I'm always concerned when I hear them say they are comfortable. What does comfortable mean? Is it peace and quiet? Is it "no more decisions"? Or is it just not being uncomfortable. A person's comfort zone can affect where they live, travel, people with whom they associate, and even their career choice.

When a person goes into a room full of people, he will look for familiar faces, conversations, facilities, or food. The person will look for a comfort zone. If they are comfortable meeting new people, they will look for people that they don't know. If they are somewhat shy, they will look for familiar faces. The host has the important job of helping the guest feel comfortable.

The host tries to make the guest feel welcome—comfortable. They may explain the venue, make introductions, or help with food or drink. The mission is to establish a comfort zone for the guest. In business, we want all the participants in a meeting to have some level of comfort. Without it, participants are distracted from the meeting as they continue to search for their comfort zone. Once the guest has a comfort zone, they can begin to participate in the event.

The comfort zone is not only a point of departure for the guest, it is also a safe haven for retreat. When we leave our comfort zone, we are in unfamiliar territory. Without knowledge or understanding of what is to come, hesitation and fear takes over. Fear paralyzes. Knowledge energizes.

The Comfort Zone

> Fear will return us to our old comfort zone. Knowledge will drive us to a new comfort zone.

Andy remembered GP and Andy's dad talking about "comfortable" and learning to golf. *"You have to get comfortable at being uncomfortable before you can get comfortable."* That means that you have to be willing to change that which you are comfortable in order to grow. Most people gravitate to where they are most comfortable. That is their comfort zone.

The Golf Lesson

Grandpa and Andy were in the backyard. It was spring, and GP was getting his golf game ready for the season. Andy was watching GP and teeing up the balls for GP to hit into the net. Swing after swing for almost an hour. Andy was having a good time teeing up the balls. But he was curious as to why GP was frustrated when he was supposed to be having fun.

GP explained that in order to get good at something, you have to be willing to do it poorly until you get it right. Andy thought why spend time doing something poorly. Just do it right the first time. How simple life could be if we just let the kids figure things out.

Finally, it was Andy's turn to hit the balls. This was the first time he had tried to swing the club, let alone hit the ball. GP went over the proper grip. Andy said that it was uncomfortable. GP went over the proper swing. Andy said that it was uncomfortable. The first swing, Andy hit the ground behind the ball. That was uncomfortable. There were more instructions from GP. Andy was getting really uncomfortable. The next swing missed the ball completely. GP stepped back. It was time to let Andy figure out his swing. He let Andy try several times. Finally, Andy hit the ball.

The Comfort Zone

Andy looked up with more surprise than accomplishment. He wondered, how could GP hit the ball every time and he could barely swing or hit the ball? Did GP miss the ball over and over before he could hit it every time? How can golf be fun? Everything is uncomfortable.

"Andy, let me 'splain," GP said. "You have to be willing to do something poorly before you can do it well. You have to be willing to get uncomfortable before you can become comfortable." He said that some people never get good at something because they refuse to learn how to do it right. They have to learn, and they have to practice and continue to develop and grow if they wish to become good at something. Grandpa said he reads more, studies more, and attends more courses since he became a doctor than he did becoming a doctor. But it all starts with stepping out of your comfort zone.

The Little Bird

The little bird is very comfortable in the nest. He gets his food delivered, has nice surroundings, and when it gets cool at night, Mom keeps him warm. But this little bird wanted to see more, eat more, and travel. That meant he would have to leave the comfortable nest. He would have to get uncomfortable before he could see more, eat more, and travel.

The little bird didn't just stand up and fly. He stretched his wings. Mom watched as he took his first flight. She was there to teach, coach, and catch. The first flight was mostly straight down to the ground. Hitting the ground is like the first time you swing the golf club. Flying was uncomfortable, but after a few bumps on the ground, the little bird learned to fly. He became comfortable. He could fly as high as he wanted and land on any spot that he chose.

The little bird was comfortable with the "see more and travel more" missions, but mealtime became an issue. Feeling hungry was uncomfortable. Looking for food was also uncomfortable. He went to his GP, who said that if you want to get good at finding good food, you might have to eat some bad food first."

Bad Pickles

Grandpa broke in to his story about bad pickles. GP made the best garlic dill pickles around. He made them in big gallon jars or in a thirty-gallon crock. You could tell when he was making pickles. The house would smell like garlic, vinegar, and dill. It was great. When people asked GP for his recipe, he would explain that they would have to be willing to eat twenty-five gallons of bad pickles. He said that was how many gallons of pickles his kids had to eat until he got the recipe just right. He said that his kids got really uncomfortable testing pickle recipes before they became comfortable enjoying a big garlic dill pickle on their way to school. With a twinkle in his eye, he said that the garlic kept the boys away, for a while.

But getting back to the little bird, the little bird would have to learn which seeds were tasteless and which ones were tasty. He would have to eat a lot of bad seeds (uncomfortable) until he recognized and found the good seeds (comfortable). So the little bird had to become comfortable finding food, every day.

Andy thought, "Pickles, little birds ... what does all this have to do with golf?" GP explained that he had hit a lot of bad golf shots over the years. There were times when he actually missed the ball. But he always knew that if he wanted to get better, he would have to get comfortable with his game. Over time, with instructions from experts and a lot of practice, he did become comfortable and a pretty good golfer.

Andy picked up the club and took a few more swings. It still felt uncomfortable.

GP just smiled. "Someday you will remember your first swing. Every golfer has that same memory. There are some golfers who are still uncomfortable swinging the club. They often make everyone else uncomfortable too. They are just comfortable being uncomfortable. The positive thing about being a bad golfer is that you are a good example of a bad golfer. So it's OK to be bad at something so long as you are a really good example of bad and can teach other people what not to do."

Author's note: That's really not a good career path.

Fear of Heights

Over the years, GP talked a lot about getting uncomfortable in order to get comfortable. Many times, fear of the unknown keeps people in the comfort zone. Fear keeps them from learning new things, developing new skills, or growing in the career path. They miss out on the rest of the world. He told the story of being afraid of heights.

On the farm, Grandpa and his friends would climb high in the barn rafters above the haymow. They never knew that it was dangerous. It was fun. Exciting. If their mom or dad knew what they were doing, they would have been in trouble. And how could they explain if they got hurt falling out of the haymow. If they lost balance, they would simply fall about twenty feet in to the hay. They never thought about losing balance and falling backward onto the wooden floor. It was a greater distance and a hard landing.

As the hay was fed to the cattle, the haymow became smaller. Because they had become so comfortable walking on the beams in the rafters, falling no longer became a concern. They played tag and chased each other high along the roof of the barn. They had become comfortable and never thought about the fear of heights.

Motivation Can Conquer Fear

The fear of heights had to be overcome. GP said that the challenge was dealing with the thought of falling. That fear could be paralyzing. As kids climbed the rafters, the fear of falling was replaced by the motivation of fun and excitement. Motivation moves people from their comfort zone to the challenges and reward of being uncomfortable. Think about the ironworker fifty stories above the ground. What motivates him to dismiss the fear of falling and walk on the narrow beams?

The Test

If people were asked to walk on a six-inch-wide line painted on the floor, most people would not have any trouble and would easily walk the line. If the same six-inch-wide line was on a board lying on the floor, most people would not object, but some would have difficulty staying on the board. If we raised the board just five feet off the floor, fear enters the picture. A safety harness, a balance pole, or padded floor might relieve the fears, but some still may not be able to overcome their fear. If the only motivation was to measure people's perception and understanding of fear, few people would walk the plank. But if we paid them $1,000, some would take it, $10,000 and a few more would take it, and so on. At some point, if the reward is big enough, motivation will overcome the fear.

If we take our example to the extreme, and now the six-inch plank is twenty stories high between two buildings. The plank between the buildings is the only way out of your burning building, would you walk the plank? Same distance, same-width plank, only very high. Some people would rather die in the fire than to take their chances of safety versus a fall from the plank. Even worse, if your child were on the other end of the plank, would you cross the plank? These may be way-out challenges, but the six-inch plank is the same. Only the environment and the perception of risk have changed. How does the ironworker who walks on narrow beams fifty stories above the ground deal with the fear of heights? He focuses on the walk and not the where. The fear of falling on the next step will prevent him from taking the next step. It paralyzes the body. Take away the fear, and it's just like a walk in the park.

It is interesting that people can experience all the emotions and physical responses from the fear of falling without experiencing the actual event. People may dream of falling and wake up with their heart pounding and profuse sweating. People faced with the anticipation of height (standing near a window, getting on an elevator, standing on a balcony) may experience rapid heart rate, weak knees, and even fainting. These are physiological responses to the *perception* of an event. To the individual, the response is to the event yet to be realized. *The fear overrides reality.*

FEAR: False Evidence Appearing Real

Grandpa often told Andy that fear can keep people from growing, moving forward in their careers, or even maintaining their comfort zone. He said that fear is a normal response to certain stimuli or events in our life. (More on managing fears in chapter 5, "Growth Is a Decision.") Fears can motivate or paralyze. If you learn to respect, understand, and respond to fears, you will be able to use the emotion of fear to help you to survive and grow. Respecting fears acknowledges their existence and puts them into proper perspective. Understanding fears sets priorities and helps us to discern fallacy from reality. Responding to fears allows us to use fear as a tool for growth and survival.

The Comfort Zone

Blowing Bubbles

Andy and his cousins loved to come to GP's house. GP had a backyard pool, and they always had so much fun playing games in the water. Grandpa would throw coins into the pool, and the kids would see who could get the most money from the bottom of the pool. Andy rarely won the game. GP noticed that he seemed to stay in the shallow area and would try to reach the coins with his toes. He also noticed that when they played volleyball in the pool, Andy always played from the shallow end.

One day, GP asked Andy to retrieve one of the dog's toy bones that had sunk to the bottom of the pool. When Andy saw that it was in the deeper water, he started looking for the skimmer pole to reach the toy. GP told him to just jump in and get it. Andy appeared embarrassed in front of GP.

"Andy, is there something that I can help you with?" asked GP.

"I don't want to get water in my ears," Andy replied.

"The water won't hurt your ears. Just jump in and get the toy."

"I can't open my eyes in the water," Andy explained.

Grandpa saw more resistance than normal from Andy. What was really the problem? Grandpa went in the house and came out wearing his swimsuit.

"Let's do it together," Grandpa called to Andy.

When they both stood in the shallow water, Grandpa asked Andy to swim toward him. Andy began to swim with his head high and his feet on the bottom of the pool. GP had Andy try without touching the bottom of the pool. Andy splashed and splashed trying to keep his head above the water. Andy was afraid to put his head under the water.

GP took Andy to the edge of the pool. With Andy's outstretched arms and a tight grip on the pool ladder, GP had Andy try to blow bubbles in the water. After a couple tries, Andy was comfortable blowing the bubbles. GP had Andy see how deep he could put his head under the water to blow the bubbles. As Andy became more comfortable, he found that he could touch the bottom of the pool while he blew bubbles. This was fun. Now GP asked Andy to see how many bubbles he could blow with one big breath of air. When Andy came up, he told GP how many bubbles he had blown. Then Andy realized that he had opened his eyes underwater to see the bubbles.

Next, Grandpa had Andy push off from the side of the pool without paddling while blowing bubbles. Andy pushed off and reached Grandpa, only a few feet away. Each time Andy pushed off, GP moved a little further away. After Andy realized that he couldn't reach GP with one breath of bubbles, he started paddling to get there a little sooner. Andy was having fun. More important was that he was becoming comfortable with putting his head under the water.

By the end of summer, Andy was diving into the deep end of the pool, swimming across the pool, and retrieving coins from the bottom of the pool. Leaning to blow bubbles was a profitable experience. So long as Andy harbored the fear of getting his face under the water, he protected himself by avoiding games that might put him under the water. For safety's sake, that was good for him. But was it a legitimate fear?

To Andy, it was very real. Had he not overcome the fear, he would create barriers in his activities. He might stay away from the beaches, pools, boat rides, or cruises. He would be trapped within his own comfort zone. Fortunately, GP recognized Andy's fear and helped him work through it. Once Andy accepted and respected his fear, once he understood the fear, and finally, once he was willing to respond to the fear, the effects of the fear were gone. This does not mean that Andy will try to swim across the Atlantic Ocean. But he is not afraid to enjoy the beaches and swim in the ocean.

The Village People: Walls and Barriers

Grandpa thought that many people have fears that limit their relationships, careers, and lifestyle. He told the story about the people in a village who constructed fences and, later, walls to protect their village. When the fences were breached, they built the walls. When the walls were threatened, they built them higher and stronger. When the walls were again threatened, they built a second wall inside the outer wall. This meant that the people in the village had less space to work and live. Over time, the population increased, and the people and livestock began competing for food and space to live. The village was growing, but all within the confines of the walls.

As time progressed, the younger generation asked the elders about the walls. The walls were built to protect the village. They reported that over the years, many people climbed over the walls to see what was on the other side. No one ever returned to the village. If no one ever returned, they concluded that it must be dangerous on the other side.

One day, a terrible storm came over the village. The winds were so strong that they toppled one of the walls. When the sun came up, the people looked over the wall. They saw beautiful fields covered with waves of grain. They saw people tending their livestock. The land was lush. The forest was thick. The village people recognized some of the people in the fields. They were the people who climbed over the wall. They never came back to the village.

The Comfort Zone

GP said that once the village people were confined within the walls, they lost their potential to grow. They justified the wall by perpetuating and exaggerating the danger on the other side of the walls. The people who climbed over the walls realized that the wall did not protect the village. The walls actually prevented the village from growing or expanding.

Change to Grow and Grow to Change

GP said that like the people in the village who used the walls to protect them, people also create emotional walls. They create a comfort zone in which to live. But in order to grow, they must step out of their comfort zone. They have to get uncomfortable, climb the walls, in order to achieve their dreams. You can't keep doing the same thing over and over and expect different results.

If change is part of life and we resist change by building walls to protect our comfort zone, eventually we will be trapped in our own comfort zone. If we accept and embrace change as part of the growth process, then the walls will be nothing more than stepping-stones on the path to our future. Example, if you draw concentric circles each inside the other, eventually, you will only need to draw a dot. The dot is the center of all the circles. You are limited by the center of the circle.

But if you draw concentric circles each outside the other, there is no limit to the number of circles that you can draw. Every person draws the circles for their own comfort zone. Some draw circles inside (within), and others draw their circles outside (around) the previous circle.

GP said that the greatest potential for one's future lies outside of their comfort zone. Most inventions and progress in science and medicine came from those who were willing to step out of their comfort zone. And like the people in the village who thought that it was dangerous to leave the village, people will want to keep you in the place where they are comfortable. *They want to keep you in their comfort zone.*

Comfort Zone
Creating or Breaking Barriers

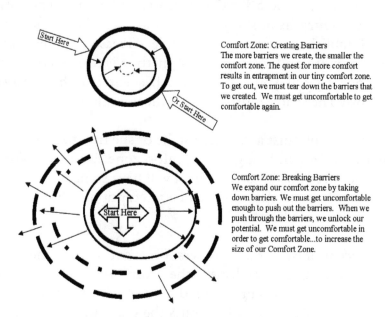

Comfort Zone: Creating Barriers
The more barriers we create, the smaller the comfort zone. The quest for more comfort results in entrapment in our tiny comfort zone. To get out, we must tear down the barriers that we created. We must get uncomfortable to get comfortable again.

Comfort Zone: Breaking Barriers
We expand our comfort zone by taking down barriers. We must get uncomfortable enough to push out the barriers. When we push through the barriers, we unlock our potential. We must get uncomfortable in order to get comfortable...to increase the size of our Comfort Zone.

Change, Comfort, and Growth

Grandpa talked about being willing to change. He said, "Change is necessary for growth. In order to grow, you must be willing to change. If change takes us out of our comfort zone, then we must assume that we must get uncomfortable in order to execute change. We must get uncomfortable in order to grow."

Andy opened GP's notebook to see what GP had written about the comfort zone. There was an interesting side note about a sentry and a host.

Grandpa's Notes

Receptionist: Sentry or Host

There is a difference between a receptionist and a host. A receptionist can be a host or a sentry. When a receptionist acts as a sentry, he or she gives directions, sets the boundaries, and establishes territories. Example: "Please complete the questionnaire and wait in line 2 in the visitors' section for someone to call you." The guest has entered the sentry's territory. The sentry must establish the boundary.

When a receptionist acts as a host, he or she tries to tear down barriers and expand the guest's comfort zone. Example: "When you complete this questionnaire, I will have someone see how we can help you." All hosts can be a receptionist, but not all receptionists are hosts.

The receptionist for a business or event makes the first impression and establishes the comfort level for the guests. Acting as a sentry puts the guest where the sentry is comfortable. Acting as a host puts the guest where the guest will be comfortable. Comfortable guests enjoy support and return. Uncomfortable guests talk about their experiences. Businesses prefer guests who support their business rather than those who just talk about their business.

Andy wasn't sure what this host and receptionist note was about. He thought Grandpa must have had an experience with a receptionist at one of the offices. He likes to keep notes. Andy read on.

Grandpa's Notes

The Comfort Zone

Lesson to learn: I must get uncomfortable in order to get comfortable.

What is our comfort zone?

The comfort zone is the area within which we live and function. It reflects our most interpersonal being, our relationship with people, our profession and self-esteem. It is a manifestation of the way we think, act, and live our lives. Our comfort zone is where we are able to accomplish or attain all the things that we want out of life. We are able to meet our personal priorities—God, country, family, personal events.

Priorities and Comfort Zone

When our priorities are in proper order, we grow, we achieve, and we succeed. When they are not in order, we lose focus, lack direction, and fail. After survival, the top three priorities are God, country, and family in that order.

God

Our spiritual belief gives us inner peace, hope, inspiration, and a better understanding of oneself and the people around us. It should be our highest priority. It is the foundation and provides direction for all subsequent priorities. Our country and government is based on the Judeo-Christian teachings and traditions.

Country

Our second priority is to support and preserve our country. Some may feel that their family is a higher priority than their country. This point may be debated, but the country provides the security for generational growth of the family unit. Without the country, the family unit functions in the survival mode.

Family

The third priority is to provide for our family. We must surpass simply surviving and focus on growth. We must build on the successes and failures of past generations. When the priorities are in order, families experience generational growth.

Personal Events

Personal events represent all the other things that take up our time each day. How we manage personal events is critical to our personal success in life. We are constantly assessing personal events in order to reach certain goals. Should I put gas in the car or buy the new pair of shoes. Putting gas in the cars gets you to work so that you can buy shoes. Buy the shoes before the gas and you will have your last pair of new shoes and nowhere to go.

What about missing an important business meeting in order to go to your child's third birthday party? How many of us remember our third birthday party? Does the party have to be on the actual birth date? We adjust our priorities to fit our comfort zone. If we agree that how we manage our priorities will determine our direction in life and our successes or failures, then our priorities should determine our comfort zone. Our quest for comfort should not be the priority. Comfort should be the result of the priority.

If going to a party is a higher priority than studying for a final exam, then comfort is setting the priority. The temporary comfort from the party overrides the temporary discomfort of studying. But the temporary discomfort of studying is replaced by the permanent comfort of passing the final exam. It's all in how we manage our priorities. Golf Sunday morning versus going to church with the family. Watching the football game on TV versus playing football with your son. Record the game and play with your son. We determine our comfort zone based on how we manage our daily priorities.

Who Controls Our Comfort Zone?

We control our comfort zone. We control the size, shape, who is in, and who is out.

It may be very large involving many people, subjects, interests, and territories. It may be constantly changing in size. A comfort zone may also be very small, limited and rigid. Regardless, we design and make all the decisions concerning our own comfort zone.

As a young surgeon, I was very comfortable performing most surgical procedures. The training program was designed to instill confidence and comfort in our diagnostic and surgical skills. We believed, and rightly so, that we were well equipped to go out and practice our profession. *We didn't know that we didn't know.* Our comfort zone in surgery was very large. We could handle anything.

As I began to train residents, things changed. As a practicing surgeon, I found that there were many challenges and that, in order to teach, I would be constantly learning, expanding my comfort zone. There were new procedures and techniques. There were new instruments and medicines. I saw changes in the professional, business, and political environments. I wanted to give these young doctors as broad an educational experience as possible without overwhelming them. I wanted to give them confidence in their skills but let them know that for them to become successful, they would have to continue to learn. *I would council them not to get too comfortable.*

There is a fine line between comfortable and complacent. Comfortable and confident yields good results. You know that you know but also know that you don't know. Complacent and confident yields poor results. You think you know and you don't know that you don't know. What is worse is when you refuse to admit that you don't know.

The first step to learning anything is to admit that you don't know. The second step toward learning anything is to be willing to commit to the learning process. That is listening, practicing, perfecting, and integrating the new knowledge into the cerebral pool.

As I matured in the profession, there were certain areas that I found more interesting. I researched these areas and became more proficient and comfortable. This became my comfort zone in surgery. As we developed new innovative treatments and procedures, we had to be willing to get uncomfortable (to find new ways of doing things) before we would become comfortable (implement the new and better ways of doing things).

Today, as a senior surgeon, I am very comfortable NOT doing six-, eight-, and twelve-hour operations. My surgical comfort zone involves minor surgical procedures and spending more time sharing my professional and business experiences with others. My comfort zone still changes as I learn new things and add these elements to my comfort zone.

Dynamic Comfort

The personal comfort zone is not an island in humanity. Because we interact with people every day, our individual comfort zones interact. We are part of our parents' comfort zone. We are part of a family, a community, a country, and a church. We even participate in or influence the environment. This interaction means that even though we develop our own comfort zone, we are under the influence of other comfort zones.

Children's activities must fall within their parents' comfort zone. Part of the parent's responsibility is to help the child become comfortable within the parent's comfort zone. Functioning outside the parent's comfort zone results in additional training or a disciplinary action.

A new employee presents his comfort zone to the employer. The employer decides if he and the prospective employee are compatible. The employee must function within the comfort zone of the employer and the company. If the new employee joins the company and then decides to change things to meet his comfort, this decision might end his employment. However, if he is brought to the company in order to implement change, then the corporate plan is to expand their comfort zone in order to grow.

You Are in My Territory

Expanding the comfort zone is necessary for growth. But when it threatens other comfort zones, growth will be in jeopardy. People have natural territories. Employees put their lunch and coat in the same place every day. They park in the same spot. They mark their territory. This is not a new finding. Animals have been doing it for centuries. People, towns, countries all have their own territory. Everyone has a comfort zone. It's their territory. It is their space. It may be physical like a parking spot or seat at the table, or it may be an emotion such as feeling comfortable around certain people. They will first tend to protect their territory, but when they wish to grow, they will have to move to unfamiliar territory. They will have to get uncomfortable in order to grow.

Growth requires change, and change requires stepping out of the comfort zone.

Some people will spend most of their energy protecting their territory, guarding their comfort zone, only to let opportunity pass them by. Growth requires change, and change requires stepping out of the comfort zone. *How you manage your comfort zone will determine your success in life. It will determine how, when, and if you will accomplish your dreams.*

I'm in Your Territory

Even though people will protect their territory, they may also protect you from your own territory. *People want you to get ahead but not ahead of them.* There is an old story about a crab in the bucket. It you put one crab in a bucket, you have to keep the lid on it or the crab will crawl out. If you put two or more crabs in the bucket, you can take the lid off and the crabs will stay in the bucket. One, when all the crabs are in the bucket, they are comfortable with each other. They think that since the other crabs are comfortable in the bucket, why change? Two, the crabs don't want the other crab to leave the group. They want to keep him where they are comfortable with him. When one crab tries to climb out of the bucket, the other crabs will pull him back into the bucket.

People are not too different than the crabs in the bucket. People tend to cheer you on up to the level that they are comfortable with you. When I went to college, family and friends were comfortable because they knew people who had gone to college. When I decided to become a doctor, some cheered while others cautioned the amount of time and money that would be invested in my career. When I decided to add six more years for facial surgery training, I was like the crab in the bucket. They just didn't understand. My best friend crabs were supportive, but most of the other crabs just didn't understand. *I was stepping way out of THEIR comfort zone.*

Knowledge is the solution. If all the crabs in the bucket knew that if they got out of the bucket, they would have dinner and not be dinner, they would work to climb out of the bucket. Even if there was a lid on the bucket, as a group of crabs they could lift the lid and get out. Since they didn't know what was coming and felt comfortable in the bucket without the lid, they stayed in their comfort zone. People want you to get ahead, just not ahead of them. They want to keep you where they are comfortable with you.

How do we control our comfort zone?

Growing Corn

A farmer wants to grow more corn, but he has to deal with limits.

His fence limits his growth.	Option: Buy more land, extend fence.
The river limits his growth.	Option: Grow in another direction.
The mountain limits his growth.	Option: Go around it.

In order to get comfortable again growing corn, the farmer must get uncomfortable, moving fences, changing directions, or going around obstacles.

Let's say the farmer has overcome these challenges and now is growing his corn. He is in his corn-growing comfort zone. Suddenly he notices that he is losing corn stalks. The deer also like his corn and are eating some every night. If he doesn't do something, over time he will lose his crop.

"I'll build a fence to keep the deer out." They leap over the fence, so he builds it higher, and higher, and stronger. He is now comfortable in his corn comfort zone. Next, he notices that the raccoons can go through the fence and reach the milky new ears of corn. Reinforce the fence and create a new barrier to keep out the coons.

Even though he is protecting his crop, he is also limiting the size of the field in which to grown his corn. His cornfield keeps getting smaller as he creates more barriers to protect his crops. The farmer is shrinking his cornfield in order to be comfortable producing his crop.

People are the same way as they manage their personal comfort zones. When they become uncomfortable in their job, they may create barriers. They may avoid certain people or certain tasks. A salesperson who hates cold-calling may delegate this task to a junior person. He essentially created a barrier to protect him from having to make those calls. He is also limiting his own potential for growth. Like the farmer, he reduced his potential to produce.

In order for the salesperson to prevent limiting his growth potential, he has two choices. One, he could find another job that would not require cold-calling. (The farmer could grow cattle instead of corn.) Two, he could learn how to make cold calls. He could get comfortable making cold calls. Wow! Find another job/profession or learn how to talk on the phone?

The big question is whether the person is willing to commit to being uncomfortable in order to become comfortable. If his fear of talking to a stranger on the phone, which makes him uncomfortable, is greater that the perceived benefit (comfort) of personal and professional growth and success, he will create the barrier and shrink his comfort zone. But if the vision of success, of accomplishing his dreams, is compelling, he will meet the challenge to get uncomfortable (learn the skill) in order to become comfortable.

He will have increased the size of his comfort zone. The larger the comfort zone, the greater the potential for success. Had the farmer just increased the number of acres of corn that he planted (his corn comfort zone), he would have had enough corn for the deer, raccoons, and for the market. When a person increases the size of his comfort zone, he expands the theater for success. It is applicable to all aspects of one's life. It can represent all areas or simply focus on a specific area. Regardless, the principle is the same. *Expand your comfort zone and you will grow; you will increase your potential for success.*

Fear of Discomfort

Uncomfortable is a relative state. Most men can identify with the day when their spouse keeps turning down the heat because she is burning up while he is freezing. Both parties are uncomfortable at the same ambient temperature. That response may be physiological but still begs the questions as to how people can have different comfort responses to the same stimulus.

People have different comfort levels to the same music. Whatever happened to Pat Boone and the Jitterbug, fox-trot or the "modern" twist? We have hip-hop and rap. Why are they popular? It's because someone feels comfortable listening to them. Is it bad? No! It is just a comfort level. We shouldn't fear discomfort. We should recognize our discomfort as a response to the changes around us. Once we recognize it as a manifestation of change, we can respond, grow, and become comfortable again.

Getting comfortable is a function of knowledge, being willing to learn.

It is very common for the staff in the operating room to be uncomfortable with a new surgeon. They may be uncomfortable because they are not familiar with the type of surgery that he will perform. They may be uncomfortable because of the new instruments that are required. They may be uncomfortable with the surgeon's demeanor. My experience has been to recognize their concern and focus on training to get them comfortable.

The height of comfort is when a surgery assistant can hand you the instrument that you need before you ask for it. I have experienced such surgical assistants, and they make a tremendous contribution to the efficiency and success of the operation. Once the staff is comfortable with the surgeon, the stress level decreases, the operation time decreases, the number of unexpected events decreases, and the outcome for the patient markedly improves. But in order to bring the new surgeon and procedures to the hospital, they had to get uncomfortable before they become comfortable.

So why do we fear getting uncomfortable?

Discomfort is a manifestation of change, and most people resist change. It makes them uncomfortable. There are still people today that don't have e-mail accounts. There are people who don't have cell phones even though there are communities today that are suspending landline service in deference to the cell phone. Change is inevitable. It is part of life. Our body changes every day.

The Comfort Zone

We have two choices when dealing with change:
We can resist change—stay comfortable and fail to grow.
We can embrace change—become uncomfortable and grow.

Have you ever met someone who is "just comfortable" where they are in life? They may actually fear discomfort. When things become uncomfortable, they just put up another fence, a barrier around their comfort zone. When the barrier is challenged and they become more uncomfortable, they put up another barrier, gradually shrinking their comfort zone. As their comfort zone becomes smaller and smaller, they find themselves trapped in their own comfort zone. They seek total comfort at the expense of growth, inspiration, motivation, and enthusiasm. Life is just another day. The only way out is through the very barriers that they have created. *They must now become uncomfortable in order to become comfortable.*

How do you recognize your comfort zone?

Step back a minute and ask yourself a few questions.

Do I feel that I am learning something every day?

If I keep doing the same things in five years that I am doing today, will it get me to my long-term goals and dreams?

If change is inevitable, do I embrace change or resist change?

Has my circle of friends increased, stayed the same, or decreased?

How often do I read a book that helps me grow or become a better me?

Does cleaning out my closet make me uncomfortable?

The Comfort Zone

The challenge is to recognize your own comfort zone, create barriers in order to protect and secure your comfort zone, but challenge the barriers that can shrink your comfort zone. The comfort zone should be dynamic, not static. It should be flexible, not rigid.

The key to a dynamic and flexible comfort zone is knowledge. A narrow frame of reference, a contracted comfort zone is a foundation for failure. Focus on becoming better at what you are doing and expand the foundation for continued growth. *Get comfortable being uncomfortable in order to become comfortable. It's a pattern of success.*

It was late. Andy had to get up in the morning. He had checked and underlined Grandpa's notes. Meeting with the family would be great, but he couldn't wait to get back to Grandpa's notebook.

D.Mata 2016

Chapter 10

Always on Stage

Andy had been reading Grandpa's notes on trees and then the comfort zone. He had lost track of time. He had to get up early to meet the family for breakfast.

They were all heading back home. Most were driving, but some had flights to catch.

That morning, Andy couldn't stop thinking about the book and all of Grandpa's notes. At breakfast, he asked his brothers and sisters and cousins if they remembered Grandpa's book. They all laughed. They remembered it well.

Grandpa would have us pick a page and then try to guess the story on that page. He would tell us a story, but we never knew whether we were right or wrong.

GP would just smile and tell them they got it right again. Then he would tell them the story that was on the page. Actually, he told them the story that he wanted to share at the time. It had nothing to do with the story on the page. His stories were always about something that the kids were experiencing or were concerned about. GP started his stories with "I remember when I was your age" or "I knew a guy one time who told me about ..." or "I had a patient one time" or "When I was doing surgery in the jungle ..."

The family got caught up on GP's stories. Trees. You're Always on Stage. The Comfort Zone. Tough Choices. The Picture Frame. Feeding Ducks on the Pond. Recognition versus Respect. Different versus Unique. They remembered all of them.

Andy had all the notes from the stories. He told them that his neighbor brought it over last night. The neighbor said that an elderly man and woman had dropped it off but couldn't wait. They saw my neighbor and asked if he would make sure I got it. Andy thought it might have been GP himself, but why couldn't he wait? And why didn't he make it to my graduation and meet with the family? That wasn't like Grandpa.

The Family Learns about GP's Notebook

Many of the family members did not know about the book. They knew GP told stories and attributed it to him being a pretty good B S'er. All the grandchildren knew the real GP and the story behind the notebook. It had been years since they had seen the book. Andy's older cousin George asked Andy if he had GP's notes with him. They were in the car. Andy was reluctant to bring them out, but after much coaxing, he relented. This book was something special, and Andy had not had a chance to read all the notes.

When Andy brought the book into the room, there was excitement. The kids all wanted to touch it. They picked it up and just held it close. Each experienced a special feeling. Some smiled. Some shook with excitement. Some were emotional. The book brought a personal memory to each one who touched it.

Andy was careful not to ruffle any of the pages. George wanted to look for a story that he remembered. It was the one about always being on stage. He said that he remembered the story but he never understood its true meaning until he became a teacher and had children of his own.

George was the athlete in the family. He played college ball and got his degree in education. He taught history and coached baseball. He attended night school and got a master's degree in education. He was now the assistant principal at the school.

Mark was a police officer, and Sheila was in her second year in dental school. Richard would finish college in a year. His interest was in business and finance. Suzanne was a nurse practitioner and had two little girls. Robert had two boys, and he and his wife, Amy, ran their own construction business. Each one wanted to see if their favorite story was in the book. One by one they found it.

George told them about how the "always on stage" story had influenced his career as a teacher. As everyone listened, he started to read Grandpa's "You're Always on Stage."

Grandpa's Notes

The Actors and the Audience

Did you ever come home from a social event and find yourself talking about the people or a person more than the event? Those people didn't know that they were on stage. You may have noticed their dress, their animation, their opinions, their looks, or their shoes.

You gained an impression of them simply based on your observation. Conversely, you were also on stage. There was someone who noticed you. They formed an impression of you, and you didn't even see them.

Most people would agree that we form opinions about people based on our personal observations or the opinions of others. We simply accept the premise and value our opinion of people as valid and factual. It is based on the information that is available at the moment.

But is it a true and accurate assessment of that individual? Would you accept an opinion of you based on the same type of information? Unfortunately, people form opinions of us every day. *We are always on stage.* People notice us whether we see them or not.

We can influence people's impression of us. It is our agenda or our performance on our stage. We've formed opinions of people based on their nose, their walk, their clothes, their teeth, or their opinion. Keep in mind that people have an opinion of us based on the same criteria.

It's important then that when we are on stage, we take charge of our performance. There are four take-charge elements for our performance:

1. Responsibility. Take responsibility for our performance.
2. Credibility. Give a credible performance.
3. Preparation. Take time to prepare for your performance.
4. Performance. Always give your best performance.

If we want people to have the right impression, if we want them to get the right message, then we must present a well-prepared, credible performance. We must take responsibility for our performance and execute it well.

In every performance, there is the actor and the audience.

The Actors	The Audience
Parent	Children
Teacher	Students
Minister	Congregation
Policemen	Community
Doctor	Patient
Salesman	Client
Manager	Staff
Employer	Employee
Politician	Constituency
Me	You

The actors are not limited, nor are the members of the audience. Everyone has an acting role during his or her day-to-day activity. And everyone engages in audience participation.

Children observe their parents and learn from their performance. Parents observe their children and modify their performance to the needs of the children. Parenting is not that simple, and parents have a tremendous responsibility for the actions that they present to their children.

The salesman wins the sale if he is able to give a credible performance. But the customer must also impress the salesman that he will honor his obligations in the transaction. Both are performers with a respective message.

As a surgeon (the actor), my message must be that I am willing to help you (the audience). The patient's (actor) message must reflect how they want the surgeon (audience) to help them. If the patient's message is that they are looking for drugs to support their addiction, then they won't get what they are looking for. However, if they give a tremendous performance and deceive the audience, they may get what they want.

Charging the Troops

One of the toughest performances that I was asked to give was in the jungles of Honduras. I was at the Ronald Reagan Medic School, an open building with long tables and leaking roof. These young freedom fighters were farmers being trained as medics. This was graduation, and soon they wound be in battle with their little medic pouches on their hip.

I was there to show them how to provide primary care for facial gunshot wounds. They couldn't do much in the field, but anything could help. They were eager to learn and anxious to get back to their comrades in battle. They marched out to an open area and lined in formation. What could I say in just a few minutes that they could take with them? I knew that most of them would not survive the next six months. But my performance had to be strong, supportive, and respectful of the sacrifice that they were about to make.

Their commander stood at my side and spoke for a few minutes. What could I say? Finally, he introduced me to the men. I was on stage. I told them that they were well prepared to help their wounded comrades. That, in many cases, they may feel that they wished they could do more but to remember that they were the first support that the wounded soldier wound receive. Stabilizing the wounds and helping their comrades get to the hospital would be their main objective. In most cases, they had to travel by foot seven to twenty-one days to get out of Nicaragua and then cross the Coco River into Honduras. They knew what was ahead of them. I knew what was ahead of them.

Did I expect to be on that stage? Actually, I had been on stage the moment they brought me into the jungle, the moment they brought me into the camp, the moment the students saw me. I could have approached my performance as just another talk to a group of students. But you just never know how you will affect the lives of other people. We must be responsible for what we say and do. It's just a moment in time. We are *always on stage*!

Take responsibility for your performance.

Responsibility—the tough questions:
- Are we willing to take responsibility for our performance?
- Are we serious about our performance?
- How will our performance affect our audience?

Taking responsibility for our performance is one of the most important parts of the performance. Once we decide that we will be responsible for everything that comes from the performance, we take ownership. Our agenda—positive or negative, helpful or destructive, motivating or self-serving—will be manifested by our performance.

Parents have a tremendous responsibility for their performance. Children observe their parents. Parents' mutual respect and their respect for their parents is a tremendous lesson for their children. It has a generational effect. Parents are always on stage.

George stopped for a second to let that sink in.

"Wow! I see that every day in the classroom," he went on like it was a revelation.

He said, "Some children are respectful of the teachers and their helpers because they respect adults. They talk about family and adults without criticism or condemnation. And they extend that respect to their classmates. It all comes from their parents and family environment."

George continued to read from Grandpa's notes.

Grandpa's Notes

Parents also take responsibility by providing the right environment for their children. They seek a socially responsible environment, respectful of authority and other people, morally sound, drug-free, with personal accountability. Children are a product of their environment, but the environment is dynamic. Environments can change geographically, socially, and by circumstances.

When parents are responsible, they will protect the

child's environment. They will make sure that their children have the best environment in which to grow. Responsible parents depend on themselves and not on others to provide the right environment for their children. That may mean changing schools, neighborhoods, or even the children with whom they associate. The parents are always on stage for their children.

George looked up and asked, "How old do your kids have to be before you feel it is not important with whom they hang around?"

Mark was quick with the answer. "You are never too old to be influenced by others. That's one of GP's trick questions."

George said, "That's right. Often parents feel that once their child is a certain age, it doesn't matter, but we see it differently in the schools. Parents have to be involved 24-7."

He said, "Antisocial behavior is like a contagious disease. It gets passed on from person to person, not by physical contact, but by observation. A drug is not given to a teen against his will. By observation, he determines that it is acceptable in his environment. He learns from conversations, movies, TV, news reports. People accept addiction, promiscuity, the single-parent family, and others as part of life."

George was on a roll. He felt so strongly about these issues since he was seeing it in his schools. He said that so many problems come from the parents, the community, and the children themselves failing to step up and taking responsibility. We teachers can't do everything. We see the children seven out of twenty-four hours a day. Everyone in that child's environment is always on stage and must be responsible.

"I'm sorry," he said. "I guess I got on stage myself. Now, where was I with GP's notes?"

George read on.

Grandpa's Notes

Responsibility also translates beyond the family unit into our professions and daily interactions in society. Our actions may affect other people's lives, and we don't even know that it happens. I have heard young people attribute their career choice to a favorite teacher, a minister, their doctor, a coach, or someone from the history book. My ninth-grade teacher said I wouldn't amount to anything, and my tenth-grade teacher said I would be very successful. Both teachers motivated me, the first by determination and the second by confidence. *You just don't know when and how you will affect someone's life.*

Dandelions in My Daffodils

I was in the Home Depot the other day browsing through my favorite section. Plants. I had been working in my garden and was wearing my bib overalls, work shoes, and my favorite lucky beat-up ball cap. Someone seeing me in my garden uniform might think that I was an old farmer who just came in to town.

If I was giving the clerk a hard time because there was a dandelion in my daffodils, they might think I was a grumpy old farmer who just came in to town. But suppose a patient recognized me, didn't know I was an amateur gardener, and saw my performance with the clerk. They would see a grumpy, poorly dressed surgeon giving a clerk, who is just doing her job, a hard time!

It was the same guy, same stage, but totally different impressions. My performance was focused on me and not on my audience. The patient doesn't know that I had dandelions in my daffodils. He only knows that his doctor is a grumpy, disrespectful jerk. My "daffodilian" performance might affect the young person's decision to become a doctor, to enter the profession.

I never thought much about this until recently. When looking back at the students that I worked with in dental school, I found that a higher-than-expected number of students went on to graduate school and more specifically into surgery. I continually coached these young men to continue their studies, to seek and achieve higher goals. The doctors that I brought in to talk to them were on stage. I was on stage.

So back to the question, is it important to take responsibility for our performance? The children will think so. The children will always think back to what "Mom always told us" or "Daddy always said to me that …" Is a dandelion in my daffodils more important than being respectful to people? Seriously? Even in my scruffy overalls, I can affect people's lives. *We are always on stage. Be responsible for your performance.*

Robert interrupted, "I remember those coveralls. It was like GP's favorite suit."

They all remembered the bib overalls and the heavy work shoes. Some people put on shorts and a T-shirt, but GP liked his bib overalls. And where did he come up with dandelions in his daffodils?

George asked if he should continue. Everyone wanted to hear more. George continued.

Grandpa's Notes

Giving a Credible Performance

Credibility depends on developing a relationship with the audience. It is important to recognize that we have a huge influence on our credibility and thus the message that we bring to the stage. Credentials, paper credibility, may open the door, but a relationship keeps it open for another visit.

My stage might be the exam room. It is important that when I enter the room, I recognize the patient and make them feel that they are the most important person in the room. I will have more credibility with them when I simply listen and focus on what they have to say. Telling them how great I am might be credible on paper, but on this stage, I must relate to the audience. So credibility will depend on a relationship with the audience (patient).

The relationship also is supported by physical appearance, communication skills, personal mannerisms, and the information shared between the parties. A highly competent physician covered with tattoos and a nose ring will have less credibility than a clean-cut, well-spoken, incompetent physician.

Some may argue, "What's wrong with tattoos?" I don't have a problem with them. But if your audience, the people with whom you wish to establish credibility, do not like them, YOU lose credibility.

Over the years, I have interviewed many people for positions with my companies. I have come to the conclusion that the candidate will be the best he or she can be at the interview. If they respect the position that they are seeking, they will deliver their best and most credible performance.

But I have had a doctor present for an interview in shorts, wrinkled golf shirt, and flip-flops. I couldn't get past his appearance to assess his clinical competence. I could only picture him trying to convince a patient that he could help them. His performance on the interview stage lacked credibility, a decision that he made.

Credibility plays an important role for the teacher too. If a teacher, who is on the educational stage cannot relate to her students, the students still get a message, but not necessarily the one that the teacher wants them to receive. Credibility depends on relationships more than friendships. Teachers and coaches who depend on friendships with their students lose the edge needed to teach.

Suzanne interrupted. "George, I see this when I'm trying to train nurses. If I tell them the way it is supposed to be and hold them accountable, they do much better. When I try to make them feel better and encourage them when they make a mistake, it seems to minimize the importance of personal accountability. Good students accept personal accountability and do better. Poor students resist accountability. They look for excuses to justify poor performance."

"What does this have to do with credibility?" George asked.

"I have more credibility with my student nurses when they know that I care about their success. When they accept that we have a symbiotic relationship, then they know that my success as a teacher depends on their success as a nurse. It depends on my credibility as their instructor."

"Don't the student nurses have to take some responsibility

too? George asked. "If the student doesn't step up and make an effort to learn, then all the credibility is for nothing."

"Not necessarily," Suzanne replied. "Credibility is an ingredient for good leadership. The teacher should be able to recognize the student who wants to learn and the one who does not. I remember GP telling me that I can't force the nurses to learn. He said I should just be there when they are ready. He said I should help the ones who want to learn and don't worry about the ones who don't want to learn. It's their investment of time and money that is at stake. It is the same investment whether they decide to study or not."

"Why not try to motivate the ones who don't want to learn?" Asked Robert.

"It's always worth a try, but like GP said, you can't teach a pig to sing. It frustrates you and aggravates the pig. He said that when the student is ready, the teacher will appear."

"It's rather simple, but so true," George said. "May I continue?"

"Sorry," Suzanne said with a wink. "You are almost as good as Grandpa. Got me going, didn't you?"

Grandpa's Notes

A salesman will have more credibility when he shows that he believes in his product. He dresses according to the product he sells and the buyer whom he visits. A seed salesman talking to a farmer in the granary next to the corn planter will dress differently than the seed salesman speaking in front of company executives at a national sales meeting.

Does appearance determine credibility? It can influence credibility, but it does not determine credibility.

Credibility is a function of the relationship and the message. It's interesting to see how the drug companies have marketed their drugs to doctors' offices with the talents of attractive young saleswomen.

Are the drugs better when presented by a sexy drug rep? Not likely. Will she have a better chance of a face-to-face with the doctor, manager, or CEO? Likely. Even though today things are changing for the better, we still see companies focused on the value of the first impression over the credibility of their message.

We are always on stage. We will always be delivering a message. People will have an impression of us even if we don't see them. It's interesting, however, that today we have social media. We know that they cannot see us. We know that they can't recognize us. So we voluntarily publish information about ourselves, including pictures of family, friends, and most important, of ourselves.

Will the information that you publish give a credible impression? It might just be personal information, or it might just be a comment or opinion. Your moment on the social media stage gave an impression about you to the reader, or readers all over the world.

We work hard to define and execute the elements that will earn us credibility. But one factor can destroy credibility and make it difficult to recover. That's accountability. *Your word is your worth, and your worth is your word.* If our message is to perform, we must perform. Say what you do and do what you say. Be accountable for your message. It will secure credibility.

Opportunity presents itself at the intersection of preparation and ambition.

Take the Time to Prepare for Your Performance

How does preparation for our performance affect the message or the impression that we want to relay to the audience? Most people would agree that professional actors/actresses spend a lot of time in preparation for their role. They did not begin the preparation process when they became successful. They prepared in order to become successful.

A famous author wrote that practice is not what you do when you are good at something. It is what you do in order to get good at something. It takes 10,000 hours to get good at something. Most people give up long before they reach the 10,000 hours. They are better than the person who only spent 50 hours in preparation but they still are not good at it.

How much preparation do we do in order to impress someone? Actually, the impression that you give will be directly proportional to the investment you make in preparation. When I gave the example of me going to Home Depot in my dirty old coveralls, I really wasn't thinking about seeing a patient.

But when I walk into an exam room, I want the patient to see me as someone who can help them. Same guy but different preparation for the performance.

People often ask me, "How long did it take you to write your book, *It's Not What I Know ... It's How I Learned It?*" When I tell them, they often say, "I could never do that. I don't have the time." Then they will never write a book. It has nothing to do with the content of the book. It's that they are not willing to invest what it takes to write a book.

I went to training for thirteen after high school. They will say, "I could never do that." Then you will never be a surgeon. We all must invest time, money, and effort in order to function in society. That investment is preparation. The more we prepare, the more we get. *Opportunity presents itself at the intersection of preparation and ambition.*

It is said that we only get one chance at being a parent. Then we get one chance at being a grandparent. How do we prepare for these important assignments in life? We get our first lessons when we watch our parents and grandparents. We may opt to emulate them, or we may choose to change what we see based on the influence of others or personal experience.

The decision that we make is based on an impression. What we learned from Mom and Dad, from Grandpa and Grandma. Is it important then that we give the right impression to our children? They are watching. You are on stage.

Preparing to be a parent is not simply taking Parenting 101 and 102, getting a certificate, and then go have a few kids. It's an ongoing process. It's constant preparation and execution.

It's sad when a young person says that they never want to have kids, or they never want to get married. They weren't born with that idea. They learned it from observing the parenting or marriage process. It came from credible people—parents who did not adequately prepare for their performance or did not take responsibility for their performance.

People emulate a good performance. "I want to do what she does," "I want to be just like Dad," "I want

151

to become a policemen or a teacher"—emulating a well-prepared performance.

I knew some people who practiced gymnastics five days a week for years and subsequently received scholarships to a Division 1 college—10,000 hours! I've seen neighborhood kids playing basketball every evening after school. Later, they played in high school and earned athletic scholarships—10,000 hours!

How much do you have to prepare to make an impression? Learn to smile, look them in the eye, and shake their hand. It takes a few minutes and a decision, but it will make an impression.

Even the guy in the mirror likes a smile. He will smile back every time. If you smile at him enough times, you will be prepared to make a good impression without the mirror. You are always on stage. Take the time to prepare for your performance!

Always Give Your Best Performance

There are two hats that we might wear when giving our best performance. The first is when we know that we are on the stage, we know our audience, and we have a message to deliver. This is a more obvious performance. We show up in order to perform.

The second hat is when we don't know that we are on the stage, we may or may not know our audience, and we're not aware of the message that we are delivering. This is the most common performance on stage. It is our everyday activity and how we relate to people in our environment.

The interesting thing about the performance is that it will happen regardless of whether we are responsible, credible, or prepared. People will form an opinion of us based on how we engage their senses and emotions. We must appeal to their senses (seeing, hearing, the smell, the touch) and their emotions (excitement, empathy, credibility, compassion, concern, motivation, inspiration, sympathy, relation).

Let's look first at a few pure performances. I saw a young man with large rings hanging from his lower lip, one ring from his nose, one from the bridge of his nose, two each from his eyebrows, and multiple piercings in his ears. Needless to say, I was impressed. He was on the life stage making a statement.

The next performance was by a young salesman in a sporting goods store. He was focused on helping his customers. He engaged them to find and fulfill their needs. He was dressed, however, more to his taste than the taste of his customers. People appreciated his assistance, but they talked about his attire.

The final performance was observed at a church service. The deacon was giving the sermon, and the priest was falling asleep. Both ministers were on stage, but one message was inspirational and the other was entertaining.

The common denominator of the three performances was how they made me feel. Each performance appealed to my senses. My opinion of the performance was based on my senses and my previous knowledge or understanding of the presentation.

The audience brings their senses and their opinions to our performances. The successful performance, getting your message across, must appeal to those senses in a positive way. *The senses are the sentry to learning.* The senses will decide whether to develop or defer a relationship—the learning experience.

In the first performance, the young man with the lip and nose rings was comfortable in his social environment. Outside of that environment, people had to decide, based on their level of tolerance to facial jewelry, whether to engage or defer. There was a visual assault. Their *sense sentry* had to make a decision that might prevent or deflect the visual assault. Their *sense sentry* had to make a decision to either pursue or terminate the relationship.

In the second performance, the young man appealed to most of the senses. He looked good and had an engaging personality. The *sense sentry* approved the relationship. The relationship moved forward, and the *emotional sentry* took over. When the performance was analyzed, all the emotional elements evaluated, the *emotional sentry's* final opinion was based on the dress style.

In the third performance, the performance was appealing to the senses and interpretation. The environment, the priest falling asleep, was a distraction from the performance. It was a good performance, but the information that reached the audience was filtered through the distraction.

We are always on stage. Even when we are responsible, credible, well-prepared, and give a stellar performance, things can happen that are out of our control. A microphone malfunctions, we break a heel, a baby cries, a cell phone rings ... and they take the call. A wise man told me one time, "Control the things that you can control and don't worry about the things that you can't control." One thing that I learned was that the more I learned, the more I read, the more I studied, the more things I could control. You are always on stage. Make every performance one of your best!

George put the notebook down. It was quiet. But everyone was awake. It was like they all wanted to say something, but they were still thinking. It was nearly noon, and some family members were going to have to leave for the airport. As they said their goodbyes and exchanged hugs, several asked for a copy of Grandpa's notebook.

It was three inches thick. Andy had to think about it. It was interesting because some people requested any notes that might be available on a specific story.

When the first people had gone, Andy realized that several of his cousins were still there. His brother and sister were also just hanging around.

"Hey, Andy," Robert called out. "Is there anything in the book about those cycles and circles that GP used to talk about?"

"The Circles of Influence?" Andy asked. "I saw something about them last night. It's right here."

"I remember GP talking to me about a cycle and circles," Robert said. "I was all excited. I thought he wanted to talk to me about getting me a little motorcycle. I didn't know he rode cycles."

They all laughed.

"Grandpa didn't ride," Andy said. "As a matter of fact, he really didn't think cycles were that safe. He fixed a lot of bikers' broken faces. He was a real spokesman for mandatory helmets for the bikers. Not too popular with the bikers until they had to see Grandpa in the emergency room."

Andy thumbed through the pages. Handwritten on the top of the page: "Cycles of Influence: Why They Are Important."

Chapter 11

The Cycle of Influence

Robert and his wife, Amy, have their own construction company. Robert worked in construction through college while getting his degree in civil engineering. With his construction experience during school, he decided to focus on commercial rather than residential construction projects. Amy had a degree in theater arts and marketing. When the family came along, they decided that she should stay at home with the boys.

Robert remembered talking to GP about his business and how it was growing. GP asked if Robert was growing as fast as his business. At first, the question didn't make sense.

GP said, "You can't get to second base with the hit that got you to first base. You have to let the next batter get you to the next base."

Sometimes, GP's examples were a little deep. Robert wanted advice on his business, but GP wanted to talk about baseball. Then GP explained that everything that he had learned up until he started his business was necessary to get the business started. If the business is to continue to grow, then you have to acquire different talents to support that growth.

He said that many people start businesses but fail to *personally* grow as the business grows. The business outgrows the talents of the person who started the business. The entrepreneur may know how to build widgets but does not know how to run a widget business. There are many talented carpenters who don't know how to run a construction business. There are many talented doctors who don't know how to run the business side of their practices. If they don't take the time to learn the business side of a practice of medicine, their practice will fail. They will end up working for a businessman who knows how to run a medical practice but nothing about medicine.

If Robert wants to continue to grow his construction business, he will have to invest in business talent. If he decided to go to business school, then he will have to invest in construction talent. Either way, the bottom line was that he would have to add talent in order to grow his business.

Amy had a minor in marketing and worked for a marketing firm before they got married. She could bring some business talent to their business. As their business grew, they added a bookkeeper, a salesperson, and an HR person. Now, Robert focuses on the construction operations, and Amy focuses on the corporate side of the business. Robert and Amy realized that they didn't have to do everything. They just had to add the talent to get things done.

Robert wanted to see the section of Grandpa's notebook that described the Circles of Influence. When he looked in the notes, he found notes on the Cycle of Influence. This was different from the Circle of Influence. Robert didn't recognize the Cycle of Influence, but suddenly Sheila jumped in. She remembered all about the Cycle.

The Cycle of Influence

Sheila was in her second year in dental school. She remembered when she was trying to decide where to go to dental school. She asked GP for his suggestion, and he was off on one of his stories. He said that all dental schools have the same basic curriculum. They vary in class size, location, tradition, and reputation. You need to know what they offer beyond the minimum curriculum requirements, which differentiates the schools and its graduates.

She shared with GP what she knew about the schools to date. She read their brochures, talked to the admissions teams, and had a chance to talk to some of the students.

"Have you talked to any of the doctors in practice who graduated from these schools?" GP asked.

He said that most doctors love to share their thoughts with new and prospective students. They've "been there and done that." He said that these doctors might have a better feeling about how well you will do when you graduate. They may also share their dental school experiences with you, which can be very helpful.

Grandpa told Sheila that if you want to know where you will be five years from now, talk to someone who already has been doing for the last five years what you are planning to do for the next five years. Talk to the people who have already done what you are about to do. Do you like their lifestyle? Would they do it all again?

Sheila shared that GP just wanted to talk about how she saw herself after dental school. Once she knew what she wanted to do, it would help her choose the school and a specific curriculum. He cautioned that the admission people are recruiters. They need to fill the slots. They want as many applicants as possible.

The Good Old Days

When GP went to dental school, there were 2,000 applicants for 96 slots at his school. There were at least ten applicants for every slot. Only 76 graduated at the end of four years. The curriculum was tough, and the harassment by some of the professors became unbearable for some of the students. Twenty-four students dropped out by the end of the second year. Four foreign students were added in the junior year. The number of applicants to medical and dental schools started to drop.

Ten years later, GP came back to teach surgery. Things had changed. The students refused to tolerate the harassment and unprofessional activities of some of the professors. The schools dropped the requirement to attend all classes. The students only had to pass the tests. GP said that the students didn't have to do anatomy dissections anymore. That was considered an unnecessary waste of time. They only had to look at models and pictures. GP complained that the best way to learn anatomy was to touch it. But that was GP.

With fewer graduates, the government stepped in and incentivized both the medical and dental schools to produce more physicians and dentists. Some four-year curricula were condensed to allow graduation in only three years. The schools got paid for the four-year curriculum even though the students were only there for three years. It was too late. Talented qualified students were choosing other career paths. The schools had difficulty filling the slots. There were only two applicants instead of ten applicants for every slot.

All Sheila wanted from Grandpa was some advice on picking a dental school. Grandpa finally focused on her dilemma.

"Sheila," he said, "you are very talented and will be a successful dentist. I will put you in touch with key people in any school that you think you might like. We will want to know just how much patient exposure you will get above the minimum requirement. We will want to know about the post-graduate programs that are available. I will help you check them out."

Sheila said that GP was like an information machine. In the end, he let her make the final decision. GP acted as a mentor and guide. He helped her find the way. He didn't push her to his way!

Sheila Learned the Cycle of Influence

GP taught her about the Cycle of Influence. When you have to make a decision, the Cycle of Influence will help you make the best decision. The cycle of influence has five elements: Relationships. Knowledge. Trust. Credibility. Influence.

When she shared the cycle with her friend in dental school, she said her friend's father called her. He was a high school teacher and wanted to know if it would be OK to share it with some of his students. Sheila didn't realize that GP was so smart and profound. She just thought that he thought a lot about things and always had some stories to tell.

George chimed in. "I teach the cycle to all my students. I think it is a simple way to help young people sort fact from fiction and make good decisions."

Now they wanted to see what GP had written about the subject.

The Cycle of Influence

There it was. In Grandpa's handwriting: "The Cycle of Influence."

Grandpa's Notes

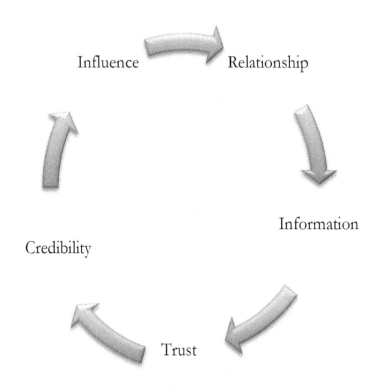

The Cycle of Influence and the Circle of Influence

The Cycle of Influence is a concept that helps us understand how our relationship with the people around us affects our lives. The Circle of Influence differentiates the people themselves. Once we understand how the cycle works, then we can apply it to the circles of people in our daily lives.

There are five elements to the Cycle of Influence:
1. Relationships
2. Information

3. Trust
4. Credibility
5. Influence

There are three Circles of Influence:
1. The first circle is made up of the people that we see on a regular basis.
2. The second circle is made up of the people we see occasionally.
3. The third circle represents everyone else—people we have yet to meet throughout the rest of our lives.

People are around us every day. The more frequent our interaction, the greater the influence on our actions, attitude, and the quality of our decisions. Each element in the cycle is the foundation for the next element. As we move through each element, we assess the value of that element and make a decision to stop or proceed to the next element. We control the passage through the cycle, but the cycle always begins with an interaction.

Relationships

The first element in the cycle is relationship. It begins with an interaction. This interaction may be face-to-face or may be through a second party. Face-to-face is easy to understand. You simply meet someone. It could be parents, a family member, or a clerk in a store. Second-party relationships refer to the relationship you develop with someone you only hear about. That could be a historical figure or a deceased family member. It could be someone from whom you have learned how they think, how they became successful, or how they handled life's circumstance. We do not have to have met Thomas Jefferson or Jack Welch personally in order to apply their wisdom to our decisions.

We meet or interact with people every day. If we read or hear about someone and we decide to learn more about them, that is a decision spawned by the interaction. The moment of interaction is the beginning of a relationship. We make the decision to continue or discontinue the encounter. That decision is based on information that we have at the time of the encounter.

Information

When we make the decision to learn more, we pass to the second element of the cycle, information. The more information that we can apply to the new relationship, the more accurate the decision to ultimately accept the influence of the relationship.

We learn by engaging with the person or by hearing or reading about the person. We get a good or bad feeling about the relationship. As we assess the information, we make a decision to trust or distrust the information and relationship. If we are uncomfortable, we have a choice of either seeking more information or breaking off the relationship. It is important to remember that it takes two to have a relationship. You have a choice in any relationship.

Trust

When we become comfortable in a relationship, we develop trust. Trust opens the door to all supportive information, which is the lifeblood of influence. Trust lets information flow to the scales of credibility. We weigh the information. If we trust it, we seek more and we move on. If we do not trust the information, then we terminate the relationship. Without trust, there cannot be any credibility. Trust is a critical part of the Cycle of Influence.

Credibility

Credibility is the foundation of any relationship. It is based on trustworthy information. When we believe in the relationship, we will be subject to the influence of the relationship. That means that it will be useful in developing attitudes, making decisions, and taking actions. If the information is coming from a teacher or a book, we accept it as credible. It is part of the educational process. When we believe that our parents have our best interest at heart, we accept their influence. Parents, teachers, and family have tremendous influence on the emotional and attitudinal development of the child. It is a huge and sometimes difficult responsibility. When this group discounts their responsibility, the child may suffer emotional, social, and developmental challenges.

Parents, family, teachers are always on stage. The child is always watching, always learning.

Sometimes a child (usually adolescents and teens) accepts information outside the family circle and questions the credibility of their parents. It is part of coming of age. That's when the relationship is tested. But with good unemotional information, trust can be reaffirmed and credibility restored. Without credibility, the cycle is broken.

People should write this on their mirror and see it every morning:

When I think I know, I probably don't.
When I think I know everything, I don't.
When I know that I know everything, it's time to go out and learn what I don't know. Or more politely, it time to sit down, shut up, and listen!

Influence

The final element of the cycle is influence. It is the sum of a good relationship and trustworthy and credible information. Keep in mind that the receiver, the student, makes the final decision on the trustworthiness and credibility of the information. For example, a young adult might consider the information from a drug dealer as more credible than that of his parents. To the teen, the drug dealer has more credibility and, therefore, influences the teen. But the teen made the decision and assigned credibility to the dealer rather than his parents.

We assign credibility and accept influence.

A sign reads, "Wet Paint." It is a very simple message. How often do people question the credibility of the information on the sign? These people are easy to recognize. They are the people with multicolored fingertips. *We assign credibility and accept influence.* We also must accept the consequences of our decision. The decisions that we make, how we use the information, is a function of what we have learned. In the Cycle of Influence, we have the final decision.

Each time we complete the cycle, we either reaffirm the existing relationship or terminate the relationship. The final decision is based on the assessment of the effects of the influence. If we choose to continue, we reinforce the relationship and start the cycle again.

George put the notebook down and looked up at everyone. They were just quietly looking at him.

"You know," he said, "GP is so right. I have seen good students make bad decisions, and I couldn't figure out why. They just don't make these things up. They got some information from someone, something, somewhere and made a decision."

He went on to explain that there must be multiple cycles going on simultaneously. It's a combination of relationships with parents, friends, teachers, books, TV, and even strangers.

GP's Cycle of Influence is simple in itself, but it is not a single individual cycle. The person who is processing the information has to prioritize the information and act according to the priority. No wonder at the end of the day, we have to just stop and give our brain a rest.

Grandpa's Notes

Concentric Cycles

Each relationship starts a new cycle. Picture a handful of soap bubbles. Each bubble represents a relationship cycle. Any bubble can break, the relationship ends, but there are more bubbles—some large, some small, some strong, and some weak. Each bubble has its own personality.

Relationships have their own personality. Some strong, some weak, some lasting years, and some that last for a few seconds. Sometimes bubbles appear when we don't expect them. Others are difficult to rinse away; they persist. Just like relationships. A stranger who offers assistance is an unexpected bubble. A clerk that you hate in your favorite store is a bubble that won't go away.

Just like the bubbles, there are many relationship cycles that go on simultaneously. We have the most and more frequent interactions with the people in our first circle of influence. These are the people we see often (see chapter 11, figure 1, "Circles of Influence"). The more interactions we have, the more relationship (bubbles) we must process. Now we have a whole handful of bubbles. Every moment of every day we are processing our handful of bubbles. One at a time. All the time. The more we understand what makes up the individual bubble—relationship, information, trust, credibility, and influence—the better decisions we will make. *Good influence yields good decisions!*

George stopped and looked up at everyone. "Bubbles? Who would think of bubbles? Do you think GP knew that we would be reading his notes one day? I wonder what it was like when he actually was sitting down and writing the notes. Did he just wash his hands and was looking at the bubbles in the sink? Grandpa was always thinking."

Andy spoke up. "I'll bet he was thinking of one of his stories and didn't want to forget it. He always had that little piece of paper with his notes and a list of the things he wanted to do."

"OK, George." Robert stepped in. "So where is the stuff on the circle that you were talking about earlier?"

Robert was anxious to hear about the Circle of Influence. He felt like he was sitting in a classroom. The only difference was that all the students seemed to be interested in the subject.

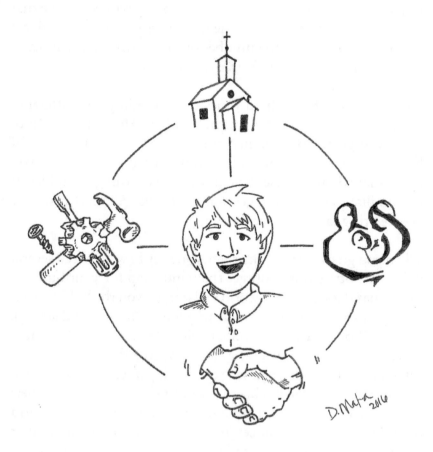

D.Mata 2016

Chapter 12

Circles of Influence

Robert wanted to see the section of Grandpa's notebook that described the Circles of Influence. There was a lot of discussion about the Cycle of Influence, but the Circles of Influence was a different concept. Sheila pointed out that the main difference is that the cycle deals with relationships with people and the circle deals with the people with whom we relate.

In the cycle, a relationship begins with every interaction. In the circle, the relationship depends on the number of similar interactions. We have a different relationship with someone that we see every day versus someone we see once a year. The subject may be the same, but the number of interactions authenticates the influence that comes from the interaction.

Sheila said she had a hard time understanding the difference until GP started talking about his bubbles. He said to think of when you go to your kitchen sink and reach for the bottle of hand soap. It is in a familiar place. You go there every day and you know that when you use the hand soap, you will get bubbles. It is a familiar place and you get familiar results. Similarly, familiar people bring familiar relationships.

When you go to a strange kitchen, you may have to check several different bottles until you get the hand soap for your bubbles. All the hand lotion in the world will not get you the bubbles that a little dab of hand soap can bring. Strange kitchen and strange bubbles. You must get familiar with the kitchen. You must develop a relationship with the hand soap in order to consistently get your bubbles. It's not until you develop a relationship with a stranger that you will be able to determine the credibility of their influence. Fortunately, there are more strangers in the world than there are acquaintances just like there are more unfamiliar kitchen sinks than there are familiar ones. It's amazing to see how GP could turn a story of bubbles into a life lesson!

"Did you find the section on Circles of Influence in GP's notes?" Robert pressed again.

Andy turned the page. Big letters: "Circle of Influence ... Don't Forget the Bubbles."

Grandpa's Notes

Circles of Influence

What is the Circle of Influence?

Circles of Influence

Circle of Influence is a concept that helps us understand how our relationship with the people around us affects our lives. When we complete the five elements of the Cycle of Influence (relationships, information, trust, credibility, influence), we are now able to apply that information to how we weigh the influence from other people.

The Circles of Influence define how we influence or are influenced by the people around us. The people we meet will come from one of three general categories. These are the three Circles of Influence.

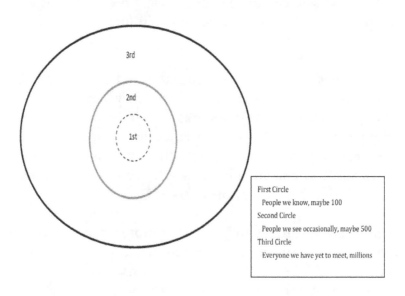

First Circle
  People we know, maybe 100
Second Circle
  People we see occasionally, maybe 500
Third Circle
  Everyone we have yet to meet, millions

The first circle: The inner circle is made up of the people we see every day or at least once a week. They are our immediate family members, close friends, coworkers, and service people. They know a lot about you. They have experienced how you think and act. They represent the fewest number of people that you can influence. Because they know you, you have a determined level of credibility and subsequent influence. No credibility, no influence. Great credibility, substantial influence.

The second circle: This circle in made up of people that you may see once a year. Extended family members, business associates, old neighbors, and former classmates and colleagues make up this group. Most conversations are about catching up. Credibility is based on memories. Therefore, influence is based on old knowledge. They knew you were always a good businessman. They just didn't know that you just got out of jail.

The third circle: This is made up of everyone else in the world. These are the people you haven't met yet but whom you can or may influence. I believe this is an important and underrated sphere of influence in today's society.

Sometimes it is easy to recognize the circles but difficult to relate to and understand just what they mean. It is not complicated. Once we recognize our circles of influence, the people with whom we interact, we must learn how to react and respond to their influence. The circles are dynamic and continually evolve. It requires a learning process that lasts a lifetime.

People are around us every day. The more frequent we see an individual, the greater their influence on our actions, attitude, and the quality of our decisions. It is important to understand that we can control the people with whom we associate, the people in our first circle. We can elect to accept or ignore, react or respond to their influence. Our decisions are based on the information that we have at the time that we make the decision. We cannot blame them for our decisions. We must be accountable for our actions, attitudes, and decisions.

The Circle of Influence refers to the people around us.

Everything in our environment has some influence on us. Certain things such as oxygen, sunlight, water, and food all influence whether we live or die. Once we get past the survival mode, then we are under the influence of the people around us.

The relationship with our humanity is twofold. First, we must understand how other people influence our existence, and second, we must understand how we influence the people around us. We are both influencing and under the influence of other people.

The circles represent the people in a given circle of influence. The first circle, the smallest, would be the people that are closest to you. There may be one hundred people. The second circle would be the people that are casual acquaintances or people that you might see and recognize but don't know their names. There may be five hundred people. The third circle represents everyone else in the world. You'd think at least a million. You don't know them, but you may meet them someday.

Influence and Comfort

At what age do you feel it is no longer important with whom your children hang around? Most parents will say that there is no specific age. They are always concerned about their children's "friends." Yet parents themselves often forget that, just like their children, it is important with whom they associate. Every relationship has an influence on us, positive or negative.

The first circle, which is the smallest of the circles, represents the people that you see on a daily, weekly, or monthly basis. These are the people that you have a significant relationship with, and because of the relationship, they have a greater influence on the decisions that you make in your life. Interesting, however, is that this circle of people has the greatest influence on you, but conversely, you have little influence on them. You have less influence on them because they already know you. They question how you could be an astrophysicist coordinating the launch of a space probe when they remember when you were three years old and wet the bed. These are the people that want you to get ahead but not ahead of them.

This is not a negative concept. It's simply as a matter of understanding. If they know and understand where you're going and are comfortable with why you are going, then they will support you. The person who is afraid of the dentist might discourage their son or daughter from becoming a dentist. Their negative influence is not based on knowledge of the career potential or the lifestyle that the young person might have but, more important, because of their personal experience and understanding of the dental profession.

On the other hand, a person may see the lifestyle of a physician or dentist and recommend that the young person choose the profession. They may not have an understanding of the number of years that they have to go to school or even the amount of debt that they will incur by the time they open their practice. They simply focus on the lifestyle, and they recommend the career. Did they recommend this career for the student's benefit or to satisfy their own comfort level?

Like the old saying, "*People want you to get ahead but not ahead of them.*" So the first circle of influence is an important circle in the formation of attitudes, understanding life, and understanding the decision-making process.

It teaches accountability, resourcefulness, respect, compassion, and developing good relationships.

Leverage and Credibility

The more frequent the interaction, the more we learn and know about the other person. Credibility and leverage are products of a developing familiar relationship. Credibility and leverage increase the effects of influence between the two parties and challenges the decision-making process of individuals. Influence becomes a function of the levels of credibility and leverage.

Credibility is based on trust. As we establish trust, we build credibility. People who ignore developing a relationship and "trust everyone" are easily influenced. They assume everyone is credible. Without the information that comes from developing a relationship, we cannot assess credibility. The more we know, the more we trust or distrust. Thus, the quality of our decision based on a less-than-credible influence will be poor. We build the foundation for credibility through a relationship.

Trust by Title versus Trust by Relationship

Leverage is also a product of a developing relationship, but it implies the loss of freedom. A policeman has leverage by his authority with only a limited interpersonal relationship. The employer has leverage over his staff. The employee knows that he must perform or risk losing his job. The child understands that she must conform to family values or risk losing her iPhone. We can choose how leverage will affect us by choosing who is in our first circle of influence. It may mean obeying the speed limit or changing jobs. In the family unit, as we mature, leverage becomes less of an issue.

Who Is in Each Circle?

The first circle, as mentioned above, is made up of the people who we see daily or weekly. These are family members, friends, and people at work. We don't have many choices with respect to choosing our family members, but we can control whether we will accept or reject their influence. Hopefully, we had the benefit of basic teachings from our parents. Concepts of family values, right and wrong, respect, resourcefulness, and accountability are the cornerstones of a good foundation.

I want my children to come away with three very important principles to guide them:

1. *Know the difference between right and wrong, and always choose right.*
2. *Always be accountable for your actions. Be responsible.*
3. *Never quit learning. Always be a student, but become a teacher.*

First-Circle Children

Children are under the influence of their parents. Children do not have much choice, and we depend on the parents to lay a proper foundation for their children. We expect our children to accept or embrace parental wisdom and teachings. It's not until they understand the Cycle of Influence that they will begin to assess the value of parental guidance. If they are not taught the elements of the cycle, they will still have relationships, but will have difficulty accessing the value of the influence from those relationships. We often see young people who stray from the family values and parental teachings. Therefore, teaching the Cycle of Influence is an important part of the foundation.

Parents are thought to be wise:
a. *Five years after their children leave home*
b. *When they become grandparents*
c. *When their children try to cover up the gray*
d. *When the grandkids are about to leave for college*

Children are constantly learning and developing. Confusion in that learning process can affect a young person's growth and development for many years. Parents have a tremendous responsibility in seeing that their children learn family values, respect, responsibility, right and wrong, resourcefulness, and accountability. We also know that there are circumstances where the parents are not able to provide support for their children, and that responsibility then falls to the extended family or to members of our society.

The interruption may be inconvenient, but the process continues. Life is a series of interruptions, inconveniences, and under-the-circumstances.

Whether right or wrong, convenient or inconvenient, the children will continue to learn. It is imperative to provide the right foundation. Given the right foundation, the children will learn to apply the elements of the Cycle of Influence in their developing relationships.

First-Circle Friends: A Choice

The second group of people in the first circle of influence is our friends. These people are the most dynamic and influential. A sibling, a spouse, or an acquaintance can be a best friend. The important thing to remember is that we pick and choose our friends. If we determined that an individual, even a friend, is a bad influence on us, we still have the choice of breaking off the relationship. This means that even in the first circle of influence, the people that we see most often, we still have a choice as to whether we accept or reject their influence. A friend cannot be forced upon us, nor can we be forced to accept their influence. We make the decision to accept or reject their positive or negative influence upon us. It is our choice.

We can pick and choose our friends.

There are different degrees of friendship based on the commitment to one another. Friendships can cloud good judgment. There is credence to the old saying, "Don't go into business with a friend, a spouse, or a relative." The value of the relationship may override an important business decision that affects the integrity of the business.

Even though it is an old saying, people still go into business with friends and relatives. They determine that their friends or relatives are different. My advice is to go into business with people with whom you want to be in business, and be friends with the people with whom you want to be friends. If they happen to be the same people, that's fine. It's tough to lose a friend over a business issue. It's worse to have to live with a relative with whom you have had a bad business experience.

First-circle friends are supportive, objective, and loyal. When you need support or objectivity, find a friend. When you need loyalty, it may be better to get a dog.

First-Circle Work Associates

Our job or profession determines the people with whom we work. We are either working for ourselves or for someone else. If we are self-employed, then we may have an employee/employer relationship. When working as an employee, we have two relationships, one with the boss and one with our work associates.

Employer/Employee: Relationship and Influence

The relationship between the employee and the employer/supervisor begins with a verbal or written agreement to provide services for mutual benefit. The employee wants to be paid for his effort. The employer expects a return on his investment for those efforts. This is a leveraged relationship. When you produce, you get paid. If you don't produce, you don't have a job. The leveraged relationship is a fragile relationship. The only choice that we have in this relationship is to have a job or not to have a job. We must ask, "Will the compensation justify the work environment?" The influence of the employer is based on his leverage over the employee.

Successful businesses strive to grow past the leveraged relationship. They work to develop supportive, motivational, career-oriented relationships. Influence becomes mutually optional. It has been shown that businesses that invest in their employees, who focus on developing their employees, are more innovative, productive, and profitable. They embrace and adapt to change. Think of the lumber company who never plants trees. When they cut down one tree, they look for another. (That's the revolving door in the HR department.) They are always looking for another tree, but eventually all the trees will be gone. The company is out of business. The lumber company who plants two trees for every one they cut down will never run out of timber (there are long lines knocking at the HR door). These companies will be in business for a long time.

You cannot teach someone what you want him to learn until he decides that he wants to learn what you can teach him.

I remember one of my mentors telling me that when the student is ready, the teacher will appear. He said, "You cannot teach someone what you want them to learn until they decide that they want to learn what you can teach them." If a business makes personal growth mandatory, it's like pushing a rope. Some employees will recognize opportunity while others will see it as part of the job. Successful businesses present growth incentives to their employees. Responsible employees will take advantage of the opportunity, which then becomes a win-win scenario. The company has better-trained employees with a better chance of them continuing with the company. The employee wins as they can move up in the company or become more marketable in their skill area or profession.

Work Associates: Relationships/Influence

Work associates come with the territory. When you interview for a position with a company, you rarely get an opportunity to meet and interview everyone with whom you will be working. We may not be able to choose our work associates, but we can choose how they will influence us. Coworkers can be supportive, competitive, antagonistic, or passive. We may not be able to limit our association with these people, but we can decide how they will influence us. We have a choice to accept or reject their influence. It may mean limiting contact, changing positions in the company, or, worst case, leaving the company.

It is important to reflect back to the *Cycle of Influence* and determine the level of credibility and trust in the relationship with the coworker. A low level of trust leads to noncredible influence and bad decisions. It's time to move on, move over, or move out. There is very little compensation that can justify working in an unsupportive, negative, or hostile work environment.

The farmer knows that plants can grow well when there is a lot of manure around them. He also knows that even when there is a lot of crap, you still have to get rid of the weeds. He will get rid of the weeds or take his plants to a new field. The crap and the weeds will do well together. The weeds will grow and eventually die off, decay, and become crap, but they will never produce fruit—just more crap.

Why the Cycle of Influence before the Circle of Influence? Sum it up. It's simple.

The Circle of Influence, the people around us, is inevitable. We cannot avoid it or its influence on us. The Cycle of Influence is also part of our daily lives. Understanding the cycle gives us great control over our relationships and the influence people may have upon us. If a person does not understand the Cycle of Influence, he will not be able to determine the value of the influence that comes from the Circles of Influence. The individual will have difficulty discerning a good relationship from a bad relationship, a credible relationship from a noncredible relationship. He will not be able to determine whether the influence from that relationship will be helpful or detrimental. *We may not be able to control who comes into how lives, but we do have control over how those people will influence the decisions we make in our lives.*

Exercise for when I talked to the grandkids or people in an audience. Go through these four steps with them. It will help them understand and make good decisions.

1. List the names of the people in your first circle.
2. Weigh the value of their influence on the decisions that you make.

3. List the enablers and the disablers.
4. The round table—how big, who, why.

Who are all these people, the people in the first circle?

Robert stopped for a moment and asked if anyone ever had to come up with the list of first-circle people. Over the years, each of the cousins had gone through GP's exercise of defining your circle of influence. He would simply ask you to make a list of all the people that you talked to every week. This list usually included the immediate family, GP and GM, aunts and uncles, cousins, classmates, teachers, coaches, close friends, and their minister.

After the list was completed, he explained that this list would change over time. You will add new friends and people from work, school, or the neighborhood. People may be moved to the second circle as you leave school, change jobs, and move to a different part of the country. The important thing to remember is that you control whose name is on your list. Whoever is on the list will have an influence on your life. It is important that you surround yourself with the right people.

GP also explained that you have the choice to accept or reject the influence of people in your first circle. They may not have all the information that you have, and thus, their recommendations or actions may not be valid for you. He gave the example like a broken marriage of a first-circle person would not be a reason for you to avoid marriage. Or a person who abuses alcohol or drugs could be in your first circle because you see them in school or work. You make the decision to avoid rather than imbibe.

Robert continued to read.

Grandpa's Note

1. Make a list. That's who they are.

The First Circle

Make a list of the people you know. If you know their name and you see them once a week to once a month, they are in your first circle. Immediate family and friends, people from work or school, mailman, deliverymen, service people are all in the first circle. They would be people whom you would invite to a family function or special occasion. It would be someone that you would want to remember on special occasions.

The list is dynamic. The names on the list will change over time. You control the names on the list. You will add and subtract names. Almost but not all the names on the list will be people whose company you enjoy. Unfortunately, some names may be of people that you really don't like but you have to interact with them at work or school. They sort of put their own names on your list. It's that coworker who takes your favorite parking place or the student who makes fun of your friends. It could be your next-door neighbor who has the nocturnal barking dog.

We put people on the list because they will have an influence on how we act each day. The barking dog may cause us to close our windows at night. The barking dog may cause us to refuse to help the neighbor when he asks. It's just a dog, but it influences our attitude and actions. We might not be able to control those names that get on our first-circle list without our permission, but we can control how they will influence our actions. We can react or respond to them. Reacting means trying to outshout the barking dog. Responding means closing the window.

The Second Circle

The names on our Christmas card, alumni, Facebook, or e-mail lists may represent the second circle of influence. These are people that we may see or interact with once or twice a year or less. When we do see them, we spend time catching up and talking about the good old days. This group is generally made up of former first-circle people. They have influence on us based on the relationships in the first circle. Their credibility may also be based on former first-circle relationships. Therefore, before making commitments or actions that affect our lifestyle, we would want to reestablish their first-circle status. We need to get to know them again. We need to put them through the Cycle of Influence criteria: relationship, information, credibility, trust, and influence.

The Third Circle

This is made up of everyone else in the world. We can put their names on our list. These are the people that you haven't met yet but who can influence you or you may have influence on them. I believe this is an important and underrated sphere of influence in today's society. We are always on stage. (See chapter 10, "Always on Stage.")

Young people see adults as role models and, as such, emulate them. We have a responsibility to give them the right information. It is everyone's responsibility but becomes even more important as we climb the scales of credibility and ladders of success. A farmer, businessman, professor, truck driver, waitress, carpenter, politician, minister, doctor, teacher, mom, and dad all share this responsibility. People don't know your name, but they know the profession that you represent. You may make the difference in the career they choose, the direction they take in their life.

2. Weigh the value of their influence on the decisions that you make.

How does it affect us?

Credibility and Influence

We assign credibility to a person when we know more about them. Once we assign a level of credibility, we are more willing to accept their influence. People in our first circle will have more credibility and thus have more influence on the decision that we make.

Credibility scale:

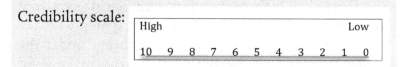

High										Low
10	9	8	7	6	5	4	3	2	1	0

How do we affect it?

Credibility and Responsibility

We have less credibility with our first-circle people because they know us. They form opinions based on a more informed relationship. It still can be erroneous, but it is the information that they use to assign credibility. A fellow golfer may judge my surgical skills on the way I play out of a sand trap. On the other hand, a new patient, a third-circle person, respects the doctor's surgical skills simply because he has "Doctor" before his name—and he can't play golf.

The fact that we have more influence on third-circle people means that we must accept the responsibility of how we can influence people we haven't met yet. That said, do we take responsibility for the influence that we might have on other people?

Using Credibility to Our Advantage: Networking

Networking is a new term to describe the traditional art of building relationships. Certain titles, societal positions, or professional accomplishments might open doors, but relationships must be cultured. The Cycles of Influence apply. Networking only gets to the first level of the cycle. Information that follows will determine credibility, trust, and influence.

Under the Influence of Circles of Influence: Negative Effects

The Circles of Influence is not a crutch. It is a tool combined with the Cycle of Influence to help us make better decisions in our lives. We are always under the influence. When we use the tools, we can make good decisions and bad decisions. Remember that any decision is a conscious decision. We make it based on the value that we place on the information used to make the decision. We base the value of the decision on the results, not on the prediction. With good decisions, we enjoy them and grow. With bad decisions, we learn from them and continue to grow. If we don't learn from our bad decisions, we will repeat them until we do.

> *If we don't learn from our bad decisions, we will repeat them until we do.*

3. List the enablers and the disablers.

There are some people who want you to get ahead but not ahead of them. These are disablers in enablers' uniforms. List the people that you feel will be your best cheerleaders. Cheerleaders bring hope and encouragement to the game. They cheer because they want you to win. They cheer because they don't want you to get beat too badly. But most important, they cheer because you played the game and they want you to come back and play again. Cheerleaders wave the checkered flag.

The disablers wave the yellow caution flag to slow you down and keep the red flag handy to stop you.

4. The round table—how big, who, why.

Pick people from your circles to sit at your round table. There is no limit to the number of people, but there should be enough to give you counsel but not too many to require committee meetings. You can put people at your table that you have not met personally but whose teachings, philosophies, skills, and talents you are familiar with. The people around your table should score tens on the credibility scale. These people will influence, guide, and coach you to making good decisions.

By now, eyes were starting to glaze over. "How long have we been here?" Sheila asked.

"Hours," said Bob.

"Bob, it's getting late, but that stuff really brought back memories." Sheila continued. "I remember when GP had me make the lists. I wasn't too interested, but like he said, when the student is ready, the teacher appears. Once I got into it and kept going back to the round table, I got comfortable. I still have the original at home, but I keep making new lists when I have a tough decision to make. It gives me confidence and comfort.," Sheila said.

"You know, Sheila, that cheerleader thing he said was interesting. We want cheerleaders on our sports teams. We think they can keep us motivated to win and comfort us when we lose. They have undying enthusiasm. They are like a puppy. He doesn't care how your day went, he's still excited to see you, jumps up, and licks your chin."

"Grandpa talked about personal cheerleaders. But I remember when he told me that I am my best cheerleader. You have to believe in yourself first before you can expect other people to believe in you. He said that encouragement starts from within. It empowers us to take the first step, to try something, to pursue success."

Robert continued. They all listened. "Once you enter the game, the outside cheerleaders can do their job. Grandpa said that the cheerleader wears a cheerleader outfit, but the player wears the game uniform. The player plays the game. The player determines the win. The cheerleader is only an enthusiastic spectator. We are all players, but we have to first be our own best cheerleader."

"But what about me?" A voice spoke up in the back. "I've always been a cheerleader. No uniform, no pompoms. Just the 'you can do it' cheer."

Chairs rustled and screeched on the floor as they all turned around. A familiar slightly bent figure sat on a chair in the back of the room. Both hands on the back the chair in front. It was Grandpa.

"Andy, I'm sorry I missed your graduation yesterday. I really was not feeling well, and I needed to get to the doctor."

"Are you OK, Grandpa?" George asked.

"I'm much better today. They gave me an IV. I think I was just getting dehydrated. Tried to run a marathon the day before. No, just kidding," he said with his half smile and a twinkle in his eye.

They all laughed. That's Grandpa. Even when he is down, he is up.

"I wanted to stop by before everyone left. I guess I'm too late. But I just want to tell all of you that I am so proud of you. I've been listening to you talk. It's so nice to know that some of the things that we talked about over the years still mean something to you. This is a puffed-up moment for me."

It got quiet.

"We are proud of you, Grandpa," Andy said. "I got your 'Grandfather's Handbook' last night. I couldn't stop reading it last night. We have been talking about it all morning. Wow! It's after three already. This book is fantastic. Can I make a copy for everyone here?" he asked.

"It's just my notes and some thoughts, Andy. I thought you guys might as well have it. Since you guys and girls are all out on your own, I don't write in it much anymore. I don't mind if you share it with each other."

Grandpa went on. "There are probably a few stories in there that some of you will recognize."

Sheila spoke up. "Grandpa, I use some of your stories every day at work. Sometimes I think, where did that story come from? Then I remember you sitting with us kids. Your stories were always interesting and had a lesson. I think we all would laugh or cry or just say, 'Hmm'! I love you, Grandpa." She got up and gave him a big hug.

With a tear in his eye. "You kids always make me feel better. I'm very proud of you. Let's just visit for a while, and then I will have to get going. My ride will be here soon."

"No, Grandpa," George said. "I'll drive you home. Just relax. Tell us a story. Tell us how you have been."

Two hours went by. Grandpa was in his element. Telling stories. These were the untold stories. He still had it. He even had that little twinkle in his eye that made everything OK.

Next, the untold stories.

Chapter 13

The Untold Stories

It was pretty late, at least for Grandpa, when George brought him home. They were laughing when they came through the door.

Grandma was sitting in her chair, reading one of her favorite books. "Where were you guys?" she asked.

George just laughed. "Grandpa was telling us a couple stories and the time got away from us. Sorry, Grandma."

He went over and gave her a big hug. "Have to get back to the kids, but thanks for letting us play with Grandpa." He smiled.

"Grandpa, I always enjoy your visits. Love ya, man!"

Grandma looked at Grandpa. He looked a little tired. "How are you feeling?" she asked.

"Little tired, but not bad considering the IVs yesterday and sitting around with the kids this afternoon. I didn't expect to stay that long, but they kept asking me about my notebook that we dropped off at Andy's place last night. He said he was up late reading it, and then when he got to the breakfast this morning, everyone wanted to see it. It must be some kind of literary masterpiece." He had that smile and twinkle in his eye.

Grandma smiled. "Everything you write, hun, is a masterpiece. At least that's what you tell me. You better get some rest tonight."

"You know, Ida, I really felt good visiting with the kids. They are all grown up now, and I think their parents did a good job. They all seem to be sound thinkers. I'm proud of them."

She looked up. "Remember the bird feeder? You weren't that proud back then."

"I just mentioned it today to see if I would get any response. Nothing. It is still a national secret. I think we will find out when we get to heaven."

All the way home Andy thought about some of the things that Grandpa talked about. With plans to enter the military someday, he was struck by his comments about the meaning of the American flag.

Grandpa said that when you see the flag, it is much more than just that piece of red, white, and blue cloth. It represents the sacrifices of many men and women over several hundred years. Even before there was a need to make the flag, men and women decided that there had to be a place where all men were created equal, where they would have a right to life, liberty, and the pursuit of happiness. It took the discovery of a continent, the migration of peoples from all over the world, and finally, the agreement among men that this was the place. They planted their flag. Our flag.

He said that every stitch and thread, the thousands of them that make up the flag, represents the thousands of sacrifices that men and women made over time. No one could stop the efforts of these men and women because people didn't recognize what they were doing. Their efforts transcended generations. It was one effort, one sacrifice at a time, over many generations. It was just one stitch at a time.

Grandpa looked at everyone sitting in front of him. "The only way that flag will be taken apart will be one stitch at a time. We must watch out for anyone who will just take a stitch today and a piece of thread tomorrow. We may not miss a stitch today, but one stitch at a time over time will take away our flag. When the flag goes, so goes our life, liberty, and the pursuit of happiness."

"Historians have said that our form of government, 'of the people and by the people,' will not last. Once some people get something for nothing, they will want more. They will vote for more, and more people will vote. Eventually, the only people voting will be the people who want something for nothing. The attitude of 'what's mine is mine and what is yours is mine' will prevail. And the only source of their something-for-nothing will not have anything to give them. The system collapses.

"Watch out for the people who think they have a better way. Likely, they have never witnessed the oppression that exists in countries around us. And most likely, they never served their own country. They demand freedom but don't think they should have to pay for it."

Grandpa took a breath. He looked concerned. He didn't seem like he was preaching or telling a story. He was delivering a message. Everyone saw a passionate side of Grandpa.

Andy remembered that Grandpa just looked up at everyone. "I'm not worried about you and your children. I'm proud of you. I am worried about all those people out there who don't have a clue. They don't understand the very system in which they live. You guys have a lot of responsibility. It's your generation to save."

Grandpa told several stories during his visit. He told a funny story about finding a big hole in his bird feeder. He said that one evening he went out to refill the feeder. He thought it was a little too soon to have to refill the feeder, but maybe the birds were hungry. As he poured the seeds in the top, he felt something hitting his shoe. When he looked down, the seeds were pouring out of the bottom of the feeder onto the ground.

When Grandpa inspected the feeder, there was a big hole on the backside of the feeder. The plastic side was missing. He noticed that the feeder had been rotated on its stand, so he didn't notice the hole. Grandpa took the feeder down for inspection. Did a deer, a raccoon, a hawk, or a squirrel attack the feeder? Then Grandpa found a tiny hole on the opposite side of the feeder. The point of entry. Someone had shot out Grandpa's feeder. Andy looked across the room at Richard.

Mark, a police officer now, stood up. "Grandpa, did they ever catch the guy?"

"No, but we had a few suspects," Grandpa replied.

Grandpa said that he remembered the boys shooting their air rifles the weekend before, but they were shooting twenty yards away from the feeder. He remembered when Andy and Richard would go out back and target practice with their air rifles. They were thirteen, and both boys were good kids. Grandpa said he always watched them for a while just to make sure they would be safe. They respected their weapons and handled them safely. Grandpa said he was always impressed with their accuracy.

They set up targets and could actually hit them. Impressive!

No one had heard this story, and Andy and Richard just looked at each other across the room. Grandpa said maybe the boys accidently hit the feeder and forgot to tell him. He told Grandma, and she asked Andrea and Marie to check with the boys.

Andrea and Marie were upset when both boys denied any knowledge of the alleged bird-feeder incident.

At Thanksgiving dinner a month later, Richard asked if Grandpa had found out who shot his bird feeder. Grandpa said he notified the police and they were investigating. Richard said he hoped they would catch the guy. He offered that it was probably a hunter in the area. Grandpa just smiled.

At Christmas, Grandpa announced that the State Bureau of Investigation has taken DNA samples from the feeder and a section of the feeder to assess the trajectory of the bullet. He said they were waiting for results. There was no response from the boys. Andrea and Marie just smiled.

A few weeks later, Marie called Grandma. She said that Richard had asked about the bird-feeder investigation. He said that he wondered if Grandpa might have shot out his own bird feeder and forgot about it. He said that Grandpa was getting old now and maybe he just forgets things.

Everyone laughed.

"Well, did they get the guy who shot out your feeder, Grandpa?" Mark asked again. "No, we never found out. The state said it is now listed as a cold case."

"What did you do?" Andy asked.

"Had to get a new feeder. Duct tape wouldn't work. Probably the first thing that duct tape couldn't fix." Grandpa smiled.

Andy said everyone took a little breather after the bird-feeder story. When they came back, everyone started reminiscing about Grandpa and his stories. The ducks on the pond. Everyone got a kick out of when Grandpa thanked them for training him to be a grandpa. He said he knew his work was coming to an end when the grandkids felt it necessary to teach Grandpa. He said he didn't realize how many times he was wrong about something. This time there was just rolling eyes without the smile.

But the best story was when he started telling us about bacon and hams. Andy started laughing just thinking about it.

Grandpa started, "It's getting late. I'll leave you with this. This is something to think about."

Grandpa grew up on a farm, so some of his stories were rooted in rural wisdom.

"Holstein cows, the black-and-white ones, have big udders and can produce three to four gallons of milk at a time. Jersey cows, all brown, have small udders and can only produce one gallon of milk at a time. The Holsteins have high volume and low butterfat. The Jersey has low volume and high butterfat. If the farmer wants to make butter and cheese, then he wants to have Jersey cows. If he wants to produce drinking milk, then he wants the Holsteins.

"If the farmer has hogs and wants big hams, he will want to raise the black-with-white-striped Hampshire hogs. They have short loins and big butts. But if he wants to produce bacon and chops, then he will raise the all-white Yorkshire or all-black Berkshire hogs. They are long, thin loined and small butts."

Grandpa looked concerned. "Now what I don't understand is why some people are naturally Hampshires but have all this surgery so that they look like a Yorkshire. And, ladies, why do some Holstein ladies want to look like Jerseys and the Jerseys want to look like Holsteins? We don't drink butter and spread milk on our toast. We farmers figured it out years ago."

There was quiet, and then they started to laugh.

Suzanne, the nurse practitioner, spoke up. "I never looked at it that way, Grandpa. The next time I see a Holstein come into the office, I'll ask."

"I'm not looking for an answer. It's just something to think about. Let's get out of here."

It was one of those "Hmm! Grandpa, you're kidding, aren't you?" moments. Everyone was laughing at Grandpa. It was time to go.

The next morning, Andy sat down with his coffee and opened GP's notebook. He was curious about some of the stories from last night.

Grandpa's Notes

Ducks on the Pond

It was springtime, and the ducks were migrating north. Our pond was a perfect rest stop along the way. I decided to take some grain down to the pond and feed them. I knew they would appreciate the treat after a long flight.

With a bucket of grain under my arm, I ran down to the pond calling them to come and enjoy a fresh grain culinary masterpiece. When they saw me running down the hill toward them, they moved further out into the lake.

When I jumped into the water, they moved further away. "Here, ducky, here, ducky," I shouted. The more I persisted, the further away they swam. Now, the water was at my shoulders and the grain was getting wet. Don't they know that I'm trying to feed them? I'm trying to help them.

My grandfather was fishing at the other end of the pond. He saw the whole event. When I got over to him, I was dripping wet, the grain was wet, and I was mad.

"Grandpa, what's wrong with these ducks? I'm trying to feed them and they just swim away."

He smiled, trying to see some hope in his grandson.

"Do the ducks know that you are trying to feed them? All they saw was someone running toward them, hollering, and then jumping in the pond. If I was a duck, I'd go the other way too."

He explained two important premises for feeding ducks:
1. They won't look for food until they are hungry.
2. They won't eat from the hand that will hurt them.

Did you ever see a new mom trying to feed her infant peas? He has more peas on his cheeks and bib and Mom has peas on her hand, arms, and dress. If he isn't hungry for peas, she can't make him eat them.

Helping people in their lives is not any different than feeding ducks in the pond or peas to a baby. You can't help people until they want your help. You can't help people until they are willing to change the things that they are doing that got them in their current situation. If they are like the ducks in the pond, that are just comfortable going pond to pond for a swim, then jumping in the pond with them will only make waves, frustrate their swim, and get you all wet.

If I walked down to the pond, sprinkle some grain along the shore, and grabbed a seat, the hungry ducks will come, check out the menu and the dinner, and make a recommendation to all the ducks that swim in the pond. They won't look for food until they are hungry. They won't eat from the hand that will hurt them.

You will do better helping the people who want to be helped rather than worrying about the people who don't want to be helped. Focus on people who are willing to change, willing to grow, willing to move beyond the past. *The past can't be changed. The future is a decision.*

There is a difference between "can't change" and "won't change." The baby who is allergic to peas will die if he eats them. He can't eat them. We must change the diet. The baby who doesn't like peas won't eat them. We keep them in front of him until he is willing to change. When he is willing to change, we can feed him.

Can't change is out of our control. *Won't change* is a decision. Those who can't change are easier to recognize than those who won't change.

There will always be people around who can't change. Physical or mental disabilities may prevent or impede change. They will adjust to the disability. We see examples every day especially in our veterans. They change the things they can change and adapt to the things they can't change.

Feeding the ducks was a decision to reach out and help. Most people have it in their hearts to reach out and help. But Grandpa also taught me one other important principle. If you continue to feed the ducks, they won't move on. They will become dependent on your help. When you leave, they won't have any feed. They won't know how to find food; they will die.

We help people who are willing to help themselves. We want to help them help themselves. Then, when we are gone, they will survive. Isn't that the dream of every parent? We want our children to become self-sufficient, to be able to take care of themselves. The comfort in the heart of every parent is to know that their child will be safe and successful when he leaves home.

If you find yourself all wet or with peas up to your knees, then it's time to look at how you are trying to help people. If the ducks move on fat and fluffy and your child likes the taste of peas, then you are doing it right. Helping people gives comfort to our hearts. It is a special gift that we received and now can share. Reach out and touch someone.

Who Shot My Bird Feeder?

I often wonder when the boys will tell me that they shot out my bird feeder. I can imagine them looking down at me at my funeral. Andy will look at Richard and ask, "Do you think we should tell him now?"

"No, let's just wait till we are in heaven too. He will be in a better mood."

Those boys sure are special. It will be our secret. Case closed.

Andy looked up and thought. Grandpa knew all along. Everyone knew. Andy thought for a while and then turned the page.

Grandpa's Notes

Walking in Their Shoes

I wonder how many times we judge people by what we see before we know what's inside the person. We judge a driver by the car he's driving, his speed or lack of speed, or even the sticker on his bumper. The driver could be moving slow because he is sick or lost. Will beeping your horn help or aggravate the situation? The driver could be speeding on his way to the hospital with a sick child, or he could be eluding the police in a stolen car with a child in the back seat. Will beeping help or aggravate the situation? We need more information in order to react or respond. We need to walk a mile in their shoes.

There is a story about the aid worker who brought wheat seed to the village so the people could plant and have grain to sell and food for the winter. When he came back, the people were very thankful for the wheat, but the fields were barren. The people cooked the wheat. They ate the seed. They were hungry.

Sometimes we have to try to see things through other people's eyes. The aid worker saw people who would benefit from a wheat crop. He failed to see that they were starving.

I have had those brain spasms when I saw things only through my eyes instead of others. Heard it over and over. Walk a mile in their shoes. We complain about a pothole or a crooked line on our highways. There are people who are happy just to have a road.

We were in a chopper on a mission in Honduras and crossed close to the top of a mountain. I looked down, and there was a little shack with a man waving at us. We were only about one hundred feet above the ground.

I waved back and asked the pilot how did that guy get up to the top of the mountain? We crossed over the top and then made a slow circle to take a look at the mountain terrain. A narrow pathway twisted among the rocks and ledges down the side of the mountain.

It would take the man and his family an hour to walk down the mountain. Why would he live there? What about food? He has to grow it. What about medical treatment? He has to come down the mountain and then walk at least an hour to the village in the valley. What about . . .

The pilot circled a little lower on the mountain. Through small clearings we could see a few little houses with their gardens, a few chickens, or other livestock. The pilot smiled. "Doc, these people are comfortable with their lives. You think everyone should live like the people in Pittsburgh."

Isn't it true? We can help a lot of people, but we have to help them based on what they need, *not on what we think they need.* When rebuilding the faces of wounded soldiers, the first priority was to make sure that they would have a face. Repair the foundation—bones, muscles, and tissue.

Equipment and supplies were limited. We didn't worry as much about a scar as we did about whether they would be able to see, talk, or eat again. Through the eyes of the soldier, he was happy he was alive. Through my eyes, I wanted him to be perfect.

It is the maturing process in the profession. It can't be taught in the classroom. It comes from listening and listening and listening to the other person. As much as I have seen and as much as I try to share with the kids, I still have so much to learn.

About the time I think I've heard it all before, I learn a little more. *When you think you know, you probably don't. When you think you know everything, you don't.*

Every person is different. Every person is unique in his or her own persona. I have to look and then listen before I judge. I have to practice trying to walk a mile in their shoes.

It's All about the Dash

When I read stories about famous people, usually the first and last pages tell of their birth and death. There really isn't much to write about. Here he is and there he goes. A few people witness the "here he is." The weather and what he did between the beginning and the end will determine how many people will be at the funeral. Born 1936. Died 2006. It will be written on the tombstone, 1936–2006. That little dash makes all the difference.

It's all about the dash. 1936–2006. Seventy years summed up in the dash.

The dash tells the whole story of our lives. People remember more about the dash than the birthday or date of death. The dash makes a difference in our life and the lives of the people we touch. The dash is the part of the race that people come to see. It's how we perform. People will talk more about the performance and less about the start or finish.

Make your dash make a difference. Put a wrinkle in your dash.

Andy remembered Grandpa saying that you should strive to make a difference in the lives of the people around you. If you help them to achieve their dreams and goals, then you will achieve yours. He said, "Try to have as many puffed-up moments as you can."

There were some loose pages in the book. They simply said, "Thoughts on."
He read on.

Grandpa's Note: Thoughts on

Thoughts on Poverty

Poverty is measured in generations.
Poor is measured in years.
Hunger is measured in days, weeks, and months.
Hungry is measured in the moment.

A hungry person sees food as a meal. He makes a decision to either never be hungry again or spend time looking for the next meal. If he chooses to invest his time looking for the next meal, then he will remember where his last meal came from and repeat the process.

If he never wants to be hungry again, then he will not only remember where the meal came from but learn how the meal got to that place. Did they grow it? Did they buy it? He will look for the source and become part of the source. Hunger sees the meal and remembers where it came from.

Thoughts on Growing Up

Some people grow up as part of family teachings, values.
Some people grow up after reversals for fortune.
Some people grow up after failure—hit bottom and bounce.
Some people never grow up—live off of family and "friends" or society. So long as they are givin', we are takin'.

Thoughts on Government

Governments do not produce anything. All they can do is redistribute, take from one person and give it to another person. Therefore, if you want something from the government, you have to assume that they took it from somebody else. The people. In order for the government to redistribute anything from one people to another people, the government must create an entity made up of people in order to complete the distribution process. That entity must also be supported by what they took from the people.

Example: Potato Distribution Law (PDL)
If they took up 100 potatoes from the people in order to give one potato per person to other people (Potato Distribution Law), they could only give out 60 potatoes to the people because they had to keep 40 potatoes to feed the people who were distributing the potatoes.

Since the good people voted for the PDL, they will vote to improve the system by increasing the number of potatoes allotted to each person. To do that, they will need more people distributing the potatoes. That would mean that out of 100 potatoes collected, 60 would go to the distribution team and only 40 to the people who voted for more. Since they now get 10 potatoes per person, only four people benefited from the new law.

What is interesting about this formula is that the very people from whom they are taking the potatoes helped create the entity that is redistributing the potatoes. The farmer felt that they would have a better market for their potatoes. But the PDL also said that the farmer has to produce 100 potatoes for the government before he can have any potatoes for his family. Hmm. If he were smart, he would quit producing potatoes and just wait for the free potatoes to come to his door. Eventually, there would be fewer and fewer potato producers and more and more potato eaters.

A wise man suggested that they might consider teaching the people to grow their own potatoes. If they did that, then everyone would have all the potatoes they wanted. They could even sell their extra potatoes to the people who had a crop failure. The concern was what would they do with all the workers on the PDL distribution team who got free potatoes? Teach them to plant potatoes. Hmm! *Governments can't produce; they can only redistribute.*

Thoughts on Voting

Voting is an important right and responsibility. Some people will shirk their responsibility to vote but will fight anyone who tries to take this right away from them. Some people feel that their vote may not count in a specific election. Every vote counts. If you feel that your vote doesn't count, how would you feel if you were not allowed to vote?

Thoughts on Protests

We have a right to assemble and to protest as part of

our Constitution. People have put their lives on the line in order to secure and defend that right. What is disturbing is when people protest but don't know why they are protesting. If you are assembling to support a cause and you believe in that cause, then you have every right to assemble. If one's agenda is to disrupt in order to destruct, then you have *prostituted* your right to protest. Prostitution is generally illegal.

It's important to remember that even though you are protesting and supporting a cause, the people that you are protesting against also have a right to assemble and support their cause. Violent protests are unacceptable as they violate the rights of others. When you violate the rights of others, protesting to the extent that property is damaged, then the protesters must be held accountable for that damage. Protesting for liberty and freedom is the highest level of protest.

Thoughts on Pride of Ownership

When you own something, when you have some skin in the game, you will protect your investment. That's called pride of ownership. People place less value on something that is free. If they had to work hard to earn the money for the purchase, they will cherish and protect their investment. Whether it is a free education, a cell phone, or a new car, the greater the personal investment, the greater the pride of ownership.

If a young man is driving his dad's car and happens to scratch the fender, he has a couple of choices. First, he can take responsibility for the damage and fix it. Second, he can accept responsibility but expect his dad to fix the car.

If a young man must use his own efforts or resources to

fix the car, he will likely be more careful the next time he is driving his dad's car. If his dad fixes the car and the young man did not have to expend any of his efforts or resources to fix the car, then the young man did not take ownership of the scratches on the fender, and a new scratch is likely to occur.

Let's change the scenario. Now the young man is driving his own car. He makes his own payments, pays for his own insurance, and buys his own gas. A scratch on his car becomes a major event. He will see that scratch every day when he goes out to the car, and he will make every effort to remove the scratch. Washing and cleaning his car is a daily or weekly event. He sees it as part of everyday life. But it's interesting that when he was asked to clean his dad's car, it tended to interfere with his daily and weekly events.

In today's world, people who spend $500 for a cell phone will spend a lot of time looking for their lost cell phone. The person who received a free cell phone will spend their time getting another free cell phone.

Free is never free. Free always costs someone else. If we expect free from our government, they must take it from somebody else. The Potato Distribution Law. If we expect free from our parents, then that which is free must come from our parents' resources. As we get older, we should be taking less from our parents and giving more to our parents.

Thoughts on the Family Pot

The family pot represents all the resources of the family. When the family is small, the two parents fill the pot. As the family grows, the two parents keep the pot filled, but there are more people taking from the pot.

As the family matures, we expect the children to move on and start their own pots. They may even contribute to the original family pot as the parents' contributions dwindle. Hopefully, the original family pot should remain full.

In the cycle of life, parents support their children and teach them to be responsible, accountable, and resourceful. When the parents can no longer contribute to their family pot, the children can contribute to the pot. If we depend on the government to take care of our elderly, then the government will have to empty the family pots of those who have been responsible, resourceful, and accountable.

Thoughts on Entitlement

Some people feel that *"what's mine is mine and what's yours is mine."* That may seem selfish, but it's also an entitlement mentality. The more we give to someone, the more likely they may feel entitled. The more they feel entitled, the more they feel that they have a right. And we know that with every right that we have, someone has the responsibility to provide for that right. The operative words are "someone else has the responsibility." The government is not a someone. The government is made up of the people, all of the someones. Therefore, if someone feels that they are entitled to something, for example, a job, then someone has the responsibility to provide that job. If someone is entitled to medical care, then someone has the responsibility to provide for medical care. If someone is entitled to a free education, then someone has the responsibility to provide for that free education. If someone is entitled to food, clothing, and shelter, then someone has the responsibility to provide for that food, clothing, and shelter.

So who is the person, the someone, who is to provide food, clothing, shelter, job, education, and medical care for the people who feel they are entitled or have a right to these things? If the answer is someone else, then there are not enough someone elses on the face of the earth to provide for all the other someones who are on the face of the earth. There are socialistic societies in which everyone is entitled and no one has the responsibility. Since governments cannot produce anything, then a socialist government can only take from the producers. But if the producers are also the entitled, then there's no incentive for producers to produce. They are entitled without producing. This leads and has led to the collapse of every socialist form of government.

When we incentivize the producers by providing pride of ownership and reward for their efforts (the more you work and the more you produce, the more you earn and the more you benefit), they will innovate, improvise, invent, discover, and ultimately, produce more.

Human beings are naturally resourceful. We started out in caves for shelter, discovered fire for heat, learned the difference between eating and being eaten, and now walk around with a device in our pocket that allows us to talk to people thousands of miles away. There weren't any people who felt that they were entitled to a cave or entitled to a meal. It's worked out pretty good over the past ten thousand years.

Andy put the book down. Something must have been bothering Grandpa with all the notes on individual pages. They were loose, ragged, and none of the pages matched. It looked like he was grabbing whatever paper he had at the moment. Grandpa was probably on a trip somewhere and something in the paper got him thinking. He was always reading the *Wall Street Journal* or a book that he picked up at the airport.

Another little card fell out of the book. Andy picked it up. It looked like a verse that Grandpa had written. No, it was a prayer. Andy knew Grandpa would pray, but thought only before a meal or at Thanksgiving dinner. Andy read the prayer out loud.

Grandpa's Prayer

Thank You, Lord, for the gifts and talents that You have given me.

Thank You for my head, my heart, my hands, and my health.

Thank You for my children, Andrea and Audrey, Monica and Marie.

Thank You for my grandchildren, George, Mark and Suzanne, Andy and Sheila, Richard and Bobby.

Thank You for Rich, Ruc, Mike, and George.

Thank You for Ida and keeping us healthy.

I pray that You will expand my territories in my profession.

I pray that You will expand my territories in helping people achieve their dreams and goals by to using the gifts and talents that You have given me and them.

You have blessed me. Thank You. Amen.

Epilogue

Where's Andy?

It has been twenty-five year since Grandpa sat with everyone at Andy's graduation breakfast. He hadn't had that good of an audience for his stories since that time.

Grandpa was eighty-six now and had a lot going on in his own life. He kept up with Andy the best he could. Last he had heard, Andy was flying some kind of airplane for the air force. He sent some e-mails and would call or even video-call him when he could. He said that sometimes he had to keep things quiet on his whereabouts. Grandpa was comfortable with that. Didn't want to get the ole' leaflet program started again.

All the new gadgets in his life kept him busy and confused. The great-grandkids were coming around now. They were fun, fast, and funny. They seemed to speak a different language. He just thought they needed to slow down a little. But they thought Great-Grandpa needed to pick it up a notch! Sometimes, Great-Grandpa thought he really had something to say that they would enjoy. He just had a hard time getting the audience to sit still long enough to listen. They had all these communicators in their hands and ears. Who talks to one another anymore?

Grandpa just stared at the screen. One by one, the coffins came down. The flags perfectly draped on each one. One by one, the honor guard came to attention. One by one. A salute. He thought, "My God. Not Andy. Andy. Oh, Andy. What happened to you?" Grandpa's heart was starting to race. Coffin after coffin.

It seemed like the longest minutes in his life. Suddenly, he looked closer. A figure in a gray flight suit appeared at the top of the ramp. An officer. It was bird colonel. It was the pilot of that huge airplane. Was that guy Grandpa's Andy?

"Yes!" Grandpa shouted. It was Andy standing at the top of the ramp. "Oh, Andy." Grandpa moved to the edge of his chair.

Andy was the pilot of the C-5 that just brought home these heroes. Grandpa just stared. Tears welled up and then slowly coursed down the deep wrinkles on his cheeks.

"Andy, you son of a gun, I'm so proud of you," he shouted at the screen.

This was one of the puffed-up moments that all grandpas talk about. He knew Andy wore his uniform with pride. Through the tears, he stared at Andy, who was looking down at the honor guard across the tarmac. Andy's face was firm with emotion. His jaw was strong. He had the face of a leader, a warrior. He was one of a grandpa's soldiers.

Grandpa saw Andy turn up toward the camera. His emotion softened. The camera zoomed in. Andy looked right into the camera. Grandpa swore he saw him wink. Grandpa just sat back in the chair, closed his eyes, and smiled—memories of Grandpa and Andy.

Appendix

Grandpa's Thoughts and Sayings

Thoughts
On Making Friends
We can pick and choose our friends.

On Listening to Others
We assign credibility, and we accept influence.

On Making Decisions
If we don't learn from our bad decisions, we will repeat them until we do.

Grandpa's Thoughts and Sayings

On Getting Good
We have to be willing to be bad at something before we can be good at it.

On Getting Better
It's not how long it takes to get to 10,000 hours; it's that when you reach 10,000 hours, you now have mastered the skill.

Grandpa's favorite
On When You Are no Longer a Student
> When you think you know, you probably don't.
> When you think you know everything, you don't.
> When you know that you know everything,
> That's the time you need to sit down, shut up, and listen.

On a Parent's Legacy
I want my children to come away with three very important things:

1. Know the difference between right and wrong, and always choose right.
2. Always be accountable for your actions. Be responsible.
3. Never quit learning. Always be a student, but become a teacher.

On the Wisdom of Parents
Parents are thought to be wise:

a. Five years after their children leave home
b. When they become grandparents
c. When their children try to cover up their gray
d. When the grandkids are about to leave for college

On Winning the Game
> The game determines a winner or loser. You must play the game.
> Preparation and execution determines who will win the game.

When the execution is the same, preparation determines success.
When the preparation is the same, execution determines success.

Passion/determination affects execution.
Focus/determination affects preparation.

On Starting a War

The people who cause the war feel inconvenience or discomfort for their action.
The people who fight the war feel the pain for a moment. Then they die.
The people who survive the war live with the pain for generations.

On Ending a War

Why ask a vet

Vets don't complain. They just do what needs to be done.
Vets don't complain. They see the big picture.

Vets fight wars. People fight discomfort and inconvenience.
Vets see future generations. People see today and tomorrow.
Vets put their life on the line. People put their money on the line.
Vets let their sons fight. People let the sons of the veterans fight.
Ask a veteran. He will do what needs to be done.

Sayings

Teaching: When the student is ready, the teacher appears.

Teaching: You cannot teach someone what you want him to learn until he decides that he wants to learn what you can teach him.

Grandpa's Thoughts and Sayings

Success: Winning and losing is a function of the moment.

Prepare: When confronting the adversary (going into battle), you are the strongest that you will ever be. You must outlast in order to defeat (win).

Success: Dreams, determination, and focus determine the destination, where you are going. Passion, preparation, and persistence determine the journey, when you will get there.

Reaching out: Go where you are appreciated, not where you are tolerated.

Principles: In matters of policy, go with the flow. In matters of principle, stand like a rock.

Nature: Don't argue with Mother Nature. You can't understand her, and you won't win.

Accountability: When you point a finger, there are three fingers pointing back at you.

Opportunity: Birds wait for seeds; people wait for opportunity. The bird that flies finds more seeds. People who search for opportunity find it.

Opportunity: Opportunity presents itself at the intersection of preparation and ambition.

Fears: Fears are perceptions rather than predictions of the future.

Fears: We can overcome our fears with knowledge and understanding of the events and circumstances that currently justify our fears.

Grandpa's Thoughts and Sayings

Success: The most successful people are the people who failed the most but never quit.

Leadership: A leader steps out, succeeds, and then uplifts the people around him.

Rural Wisdom: You can't teach a pig to sing. It frustrates you and aggravates the pig.